PRAISE FOR QUA

M000247581

"I'm often asked by dads: How can I help my son get D1 offers? Hard work is No. 1. And now I'm adding: Read *Quarterback Dads*. My longtime friend Teddy Greenstein runs you through the do's and don'ts — and does it in the same entertaining style he brought to his work at the *Chicago Tribune*."

— Pat Fitzgerald, 2020 National Coach of the Year at
Northwestern and Quarterback Dad

"There are plenty of books and videos that claim to tell you how to raise a star athlete. This book performs a much greater service: It also tells you how *not* to do it. Teddy Greenstein has written a book that any loving sports parent would be wise to read."

— Michael Rosenberg, Senior Writer, Sports Illustrated

"Quarterback Dads have suddenly emerged as the most important power brokers in college football. With the sport undergoing whole-sale change, Teddy Greenstein gives you an unvarnished look at the fathers and sons who have shaped — and are shaping — the next generation at the most important position in sports."

— Pete Thamel, College Football Senior Writer, ESPN

"Teddy Greenstein has tackled a subject that needs to be addressed. He has done a wonderful job revealing the issues with Quarterback Dads. As the father of a son with aspirations, this is a must-read!"

— Greg Vandagriff, Georgia state championship high school coach
and father of University of Georgia QB Brock Vandagriff

"The making of a quarterback comes in many shapes, forms and sizes; however, there's one common thread — the impact of their dad. Teddy brings to light entertaining stories and lessons from some of the all-time greatest quarterbacks. I hope you enjoy *Quarterback Dads* as much as I did and remember that behind every great quarterback is a great dad!"

— Brady Quinn, Fox Sports analyst, former NFL quarterback and Johnny Unitas Golden Arm Award winner at Notre Dame

"In today's world there is a premium on quality work from genuine people of high integrity. Teddy continues to be the same guy who first interviewed me almost 20 years ago. His informative book applies to all aspects of leadership."

— Bret Bielema, University of Illinois head coach and 2006 Big Ten Coach of the Year at Wisconsin

"The chaos of college football in 2022 is merely a symptom of larger problems, and *Quarterback Dads* gets right to the heart of one of those problems. Teddy Greenstein's in-depth look at the guys behind the guys is a fascinating case study on human behavior and the power dynamics within America's favorite sport. It is a great read for dads, and, just as importantly, a great read for coaches who are trying to better understand their players' dads."

— Matt Fortuna, The Athletic college football writer and 2019 President of The Football Writers Association of America

"This book gives fascinating insight into the dads who try to balance their thirst for athletic success with their intense love for their sons."

— Allen Trieu, Midwest Football Recruiting Analyst, 247Sports

QUARTERBACK DADS™

WILD TALES FROM THE FIELD

WISE WORDS FOR PLAYERS & PARENTS

TEDDY GREENSTEIN

WITH **DONOVAN DOOLEY**

INTERVIEWS WITH ARCHIE MANNING, KURT WARNER,
TODD MARINOVICH, WARREN MOON & MANY MORE.

To my original fans, Gloria and Marty.
To my youngest fans, Elle and Emmy.
And to my beautiful wife, Nori,
who read every word of the
manuscript between naps.

FROM THE AUTHORS

Check out QuarterbackDads.com for merch, visuals, information on events and Q&As with QB Dads. And if you have a Quarterback Dad story worth sharing, we'd love to hear it. Maybe we'll include yours in the sequel!

-TG and DD

TABLE OF CONTENTS

AUTHORS

Teddy Greenstein covered college football at the Chicago Tribune for two decades and appeared regularly on the Big Ten Network before becoming Senior Editor at PointsBet, an online sportsbook. He won the 2017 Lisagor Award for writing Chicago's best sports story, a behind-the-scenes piece on Big Ten basketball referees. He's a New York City native, a Northwestern alumnus, a soccer dad to daughters Elle and Emmy and husband to Nori, who goes by #sportslovingwife on Twitter. Follow the author @teddygreenstein. This is his first book.

Donovan Dooley quarterbacked St. Martin de Porres High School to a Michigan state championship and coached at Albion College before founding Quarterback University. Bleacher Report recognized him as one of the country's top 10 private quarterback coaches. More than 100 of his pupils have received full college scholarships, and he currently trains the nation's top-ranked QB in the Class of 2025. Follow him on Twitter @QuarterbackUniv.

INTRODUCTION

For years I likened writing a book to covering the Olympics. I had little interest in being away from home for three-plus weeks in the summer. Plus I'm not a big synchronized swimming guy. But is a sportswriting career complete without chronicling a Dream Team and the dreams of a teenage gymnast?

Same goes for a book. It's such a massive undertaking for what can amount to prison wages. And the real work begins after publication. Pushing my friends to promote my book and have me on their podcasts? Ugh. Not my thing.

Then again: How gratifying would it be to see my own name on my bookshelf? To produce something with permanence that my kids or grandkids (no pressure, Elle and Emmy) can thumb through after I'm gone?

I covered the Rio Games for the Chicago Tribune in 2016. And loved it. Four years later a friend texted me: "Random question: My son has a QB coach who has some great QB dad stories and needs a ghostwriter. Any ideas?"

Yeah, I have an idea — me!

Football is America's No. 1 sport and my favorite to cover. Quarterback is its glamour position. Quarterback Dads are black, white, rich and poor. More than 60 million American kids, including my soccer-playing daughters, participate in youth sports. And, hey, maybe if a global pandemic breaks out, I'll have some extra time.

So I said yes. By month's end, we had a plan. First priority, to meet Donovan Dooley, the private trainer savvy enough to register

QuarterbackDads.com. He has the sweetest laugh — and a cool back-story about his own demanding pops. Most important, he remembers details about seemingly every interaction with every zany dad.

He once handed out notecards to aspiring QBs and asked them what they wished they could tell their parents.

Coach hates you. Now I have no shot.

I wish I could tell you I wanna quit. My arm kills.

"Quarterback Dads," Dooley says, "struggle to realize it's a game."

They love their sons. They love football. But too often, they overdo it.

In this book, you'll hear from a dad who says his 14-year-old can become "the LeBron James" of football. Another who let his 13-year-old drive to the gym. Another who tweets so relentlessly, his son blocked him. And one who created a three-minute hype video of his kid for Facebook. When he was 6.

"You'll 'friend' a kid," one college football coach says, "and the next day, you get a friend request from the dad."

The word "bad" appears in this book more than a dozen times. But Jim McCarthy, whose son J.J. is vying to be the starter at Michigan in 2022, prefers a different descriptor for the Quarterback Dads who make him wince: "Uneducated."

These pages can provide that education. Quarterback Dads can heed the message of the great Archie Manning, who says football is "like a yo-yo," so appreciate the ups and downs. Rick Neuheisel recommends Quarterback Dads sit far from the field because "you're gonna say things you cannot believe would come out of your mouth."

Joel Klatt and Brady Quinn are adamant that young athletes resist the urge to specialize. Play shortstop. Play point guard. Play tag.

Illinois coach Bret Bielema suggests young QBs work on their communication skills — even acting. Northwestern's Pat Fitzgerald says it's essential to build a relationship with your son so "you'll know when it's time to push, when it's time to hug and when it's time to give 'em a kick in the britches."

Phil Simms offers a contrarian take on the role dads should play in the college recruiting process. And Todd Marinovich, who wasn't afforded a childhood by his famously relentless Quarterback Dad, reflects on the challenges of handling his own football-crazed son.

If you like the book, I hope you'll follow me on Twitter @teddygreenstein and Donovan @QuarterbackUniv and check out our content at QuarterbackDads.com. We have big plans. Some of the dads in this book are ready to dispense advice in Q&As and live video chats. Maybe you'll even see them in a streaming series.

Let's also remember to salute these dads, even the ones who think it's kosher to shriek from the stands or crash Zoom calls with their son's quarterback coach. These might be the same dads who work two jobs to pay for private training or flights to a showcase three time zones away.

"When a kid decides he has a dream and is willing to work for it, you turn over whatever resources you have," says Carl Williams, who advised son Caleb on his transfer from Oklahoma to USC. "As a parent you make the investment, you adjust your life. Honestly, it doesn't matter if you have to refinance or take out a second mortgage. If you want uncommon results, you have to do uncommon things."

With quarterback dads, everything is uncommon.

CHAPTER 1

THE SACRIFICING QUARTERBACK DAD

The winding roads of Scottsdale lead to a residence that cannot accurately be described as a house. That would be like saying Dak Prescott's job is to take snaps.

Kurt Warner's Arizona property contains a full basketball court, a nine-hole putting green and enough pool space for the entire cast of Cirque du Soleil. But none of those features explains the lineup of cars and SUVs outside the complex on a Saturday in May.

Fathers, sons and a few moms have arrived because of the most jaw-dropping aspect of the property — a 50-yard football field with WOLVES painted in the south end zone. It's where Warner, on the final day of the 2021 NFL draft, will tutor a crop of gunslingers with outsized dreams.

As the tall, young and lean quarterbacks warm up their throwing shoulders, a figure wearing orange and blue emerges. He's the biggest guy here. He has hair on his legs. It's Brandon Peters, the starter at Illinois.

Peters is last to arrive, but he's not late. It's 5:57 a.m.

Donovan Dooley arranged for the 6 a.m. workout by taking a blind stab on Twitter. Warner said sure, come on over. He loves teaching the game and will spend an hour dissecting a single play on his digital whiteboard.

The Michigan-based Dooley tutors quarterbacks and tolerates

Quarterback Dads. He has so much experience dealing with unrealistic, overbearing and just plain nutty Quarterback Dads, he has come up with more than a dozen descriptors.

The Braggin' Dad. The "We" Dad. The Jealous Dad. The Demonstrating Dad.

"I used to get frustrated with the Quarterback Dads," Dooley says. "Now I feel sorry for them. They don't know what they don't know. They're not educated."

Not to be a Braggin' Author, but this book can serve as an education.

Many Quarterback Dads have a bottomless pit of questions: Should I coach my son? Can I trust his youth or high school coach? Should I hire a private tutor? Should I have him switch high schools if he's second string? Should I run his social media? How often should I post? Should I anonymously rip his high school coach on a message board? (That happens. Sadly.)

"Quarterback Dads struggle with shared accountability — and they struggle to realize they are not the coach or decision maker," Dooley says. "A lot of dads have what I call cranberry-lens glasses. They only see the good, so their perspective becomes flawed."

Dooley recalls the dad who told him: *We're going to send you a list of schools we're interested in. Now send me the list of schools that are interested in my kid.*

"I just did," Dooley replied.

Where's the list?

"I sent it to you already."

What do you mean? I didn't get a text from you.

"Exactly. Nobody is interested. Your kid hasn't done anything yet."

That note went to the Not-In-Touch-With-Reality Dad. The one sending clips to Dooley of his son's flag football games.

"They want the best for their children," Dooley says, "but ultimately they end up hurting their kids."

One of the dads documented in these pages flies a drone during 7-on-7 workouts to gather video footage for a highlights package on Instagram. One is so active on social media that his firstborn son blocks him. Another moved with his son from Canada to the United States — temporarily splitting his family — with the hope of earning a college scholarship.

His name is Ross Viotto, and son Drew received offers from Syracuse, Central Michigan and Bowling Green before he started his first high school game.

"Every Quarterback Dad will tell you he is not crazy," Ross says, "but all of us are in our own way. You have to be. You have to be passionate about the position. You have to live it. I'd like to think of myself as a more rational Quarterback Dad, if there's such a thing."

Minutes after observing Warner talk to a group that included his son, Ross says: "The money, the time, the sacrifices ... Drew has missed Easters and Christmases at home. But look where we are now. How many kids get to train with a Hall of Famer?"

Ross grew up as a rare breed: a football-craving Canadian. He was raised in the Ontario town of Sault Ste. Marie, separated from Michigan's Upper Peninsula by the St. Marys River.

"Nobody in my family loved football," he says. "Nobody liked sports. At 5 years old I remember watching Michigan State-Michigan. I fell in love."

A lumberjack of a man, Ross played quarterback at Carleton University, the Ottawa school that has produced dozens of CFL players. The capacity of the "stadium" is 3,500.

"I'm not crapping on Canada," he says, "but hockey is their thing."

Once Drew began showing promise as a quarterback, Ross was unsure of what to do. He read a newspaper story about Christian Veilleux, who took an unusual route to big-time college football. Raised near Ottawa, Veilleux completed his college prep in Maryland at The Bullis

School, which produced Dwayne Haskins. Veilleux showed so much promise, Clemson and Michigan offered scholarships before he selected and enrolled at Penn State in January 2021.

"I called Christian's dad," Ross says, "and he told me: There's a quarterback trainer four and a half hours from you — Donovan Dooley. Check him out."

Ross and Drew made the 700-mile round-trip drive once a month. And then every other weekend. Dooley initially viewed Drew as a "lump of clay," but as he developed, Ross wondered whether he had a future college quarterback sleeping under his roof. Could Drew develop enough to earn a scholarship?

To make that happen, the reality was as raw as a winter day in Thunder Bay. Ross persuaded his wife to split the family in the summer of 2018. He and Drew would move to suburban Detroit so Drew could attend Walled Lake Western, a school of 1,300 that sounds Canadian but isn't. Ross' wife and daughter managed to join them in the summer of 2021.

Dooley calls it a story of sacrifice and financial strain. Family friends called it something else.

"They thought I was nuts," Ross says. "What do you mean you're moving your family? Well, I was taught to give your kids a better opportunity than what you had — as long as they want it. I didn't force him. I'm a huge football fan, so I did guide him in that right direction. He's eating it up; he's loving it."

Two other father-son combos made the trek from the Midwest to Warner's compound in Scottsdale: J.R. and Trae Taylor came from Chicago's northwest suburbs, and Jay and Bryce Underwood flew in from Detroit.

"For my son to have this opportunity," Jay Underwood says, "is amazing."

More amazing is what transpired June 6, 2021, when Bryce tweeted out some news: "Blessed To receive an offer from the University of Michigan #GoBlue."

Why so incredible? Bryce received it at age 13. Yup, before he took a snap or pop quiz at Belleville High School in Michigan. That was his fourth offer following Kentucky, Marshall and Michigan State. Notre Dame joined the party in January 2022, shortly before MaxPreps declared Underwood the National Freshman of the Year, joining a heralded list that includes Jabrill Peppers (2010), Nick Bosa (2012), Trevor Lawrence (2014) and Arch Manning (2019).

I interviewed Bryce on the night he received the Kentucky offer, his first, and it barely came up in conversation: "I don't even know how to celebrate it."

While Bryce has a relaxed, too-cool-for-school vibe, his dad was thrilled to be in the company of Warner, the MVP of Super Bowl XXXIV: "To put him in this climate and watch him grow and absorb all the information is just amazing."

Jay's enthusiasm is endearing, but in the early days it bubbled over, threatening to spoil the father-son relationship. Now he's what you would call a Reformed Quarterback Dad.

As proof, consider the selection of Bryce's high school. Jay and his wife wanted to relocate to Houston, where she has family. Start fresh, Jay says, build up his name. But Bryce chose Belleville, which is about halfway between Detroit and Ann Arbor.

"With how hands-on and controlling I was, I wouldn't have allowed that to happen," Jay says, referring to his old self. "I thought I knew what was best for him. But as I get older and he gets older, I understand he has to take a step forward for his own future. I just have to support him."

Jay says he blessed the Belleville decision once the coach, Jermain Crowell, promised not to give Bryce any special treatment. Challenge my son, Jay told him. Treat him like he's at the bottom of the barrel. That will make him work harder.

Years ago, Jay says, about 90% of their conversations centered around football. Now it's more like 30%, freeing up time to talk about father-son stuff. That has strengthened the relationship. But like every teen-parent relationship, there are cracks.

With so many colleges already coming after Bryce, I asked Jay about the family's philosophy on picking a school.

"We're fighting about that right now," he says.

CHAPTER 2

WHAT IF I CRITIQUED YOU, DAD?

The inspiration for this book came at an unlikely place — a restroom.

Donovan Dooley was relieving himself between sessions of a camp in Eagle Village, Mich., three hours outside Detroit. The boonies. Dooley's mission was to assemble 50 young quarterbacks, black and white, and have the inner-city kids find common ground with the suburbanites.

He remembers two kids from opposite backgrounds bonding over the prospect of eating chili cheese fries at Coney Island, where the dogs cost just $2.35.

"Hey, Mom," a suburban kid said, "can Marquan come over to the house?"

"Who is Marquan?" she replied.

But that's not what made the 2014 session truly stand out.

Dooley was in the men's room when he overheard one dad say to another: "My kid is gonna win the MVP of this camp. It's no competition. My son has the pedigree."

The pedigree? Was he talking about a thoroughbred or a 14-year-old boy?

A lightbulb formed over Dooley's head.

"I'm looking at dads in the hallway wearing sweatshirts with their kid's name on the back," he said. "I'm overhearing dads talk about other people's kids. Impromptu, I just did it."

He asked one of the camp administrators to go to CVS to buy index cards and pens.

He asked the parents to disperse. Only kids and coaches could stay. Dooley distributed the 3x5 cards and pens and gave these instructions: "Whatever you'd like to say to your parents or guardian, put it on the card. This is a venting moment. Or it can be: Dad, I love you."

These are some of the messages that flowed:

I'm not starting because of you and you know it.

You never played and you still tell me every damn day how to improve.

Coach Dooley traveled to us. And you embarrassed me. Thanks.

Ooooh, boy. Dooley reads them now and shudders.

I'm gonna be better than you. Remember two years ago, you said I couldn't be.

Mom you don't know football. Stop!!!

Coach hates you. Now I have no shot.

I wish I could tell you I wanna quit. My arm kills.

They were not all like this. Many expressed love and appreciation for the sacrifices their parents made.

But for each one that made Dooley smile, there was another that made him cringe.

Dad, you critique my game. What if I critiqued you as a Dad, Mr. Part-Time job?

You've made my mom become just like you.

Dooley's interpretation of that one: "The dad is crazy as hell, always talking about how his son needs to compete. The mom was the nurturer and now she is also asking: Why isn't my kid getting the (recruiting) stars? Why isn't he being recruited?"

Those types of parents do not understand Dooley's mantra, which goes like this: "Football is part of your life. Even if you're lucky enough to have a pro career, you might be done at 26. What are you going to do with the rest of your life? So enjoy it, compete and have fun."

Little about the messages on the index cards conveyed fun. What came across was that many parents, especially the dads, had zapped their sons' joy from football. The sport had become a means to an end — the end being a college scholarship or pro career — rather than a healthy diversion, a way to compete, to get in shape and to make friends.

The episode changed how Dooley handles Quarterback Dads.

Dooley's own father was just as blunt. *Make the play*, he'd yell from the stands.

Make the throw. You're better than that. If you don't want to do this shit, we can take your ass home.

"My dad was crazy as hell," Dooley says. "He'd say: 'Turn this shit up a notch.' It fired me up."

The modern Quarterback Dad is also loco but in a different sense. Rather than threaten to go all Woody Hayes on his kid, his tendency is to pump up his son. If his kid is not thriving, he doesn't point the thumb inward. He points the finger.

You're coaching this play wrong. Your line isn't blocking. Your receivers need to get open.

"Quarterback Dads struggle to realize it's a game," Dooley says. "And in this game, you can win or you can lose. There are lessons in both. They lose sight of this being a small portion of their life. The household becomes tense. They lose the fun and sometimes they even lose the household. The son loses his true father, who should be raising a young man.

"Some dads are watching film as if *they* are the quarterback. You go on Hudl and you see 33 hours of film (have been watched). The kid has watched six hours and the dad has watched the whole thing. Then he calls the coach and says: 'I saw what you guys did wrong.' And the dad was a hockey player!"

Dooley has trained more than 300 players. An avid note taker, he has filled notebooks with thoughts, quips, absurd tales and ridiculous requests from Quarterback Dads. They are contained in this book.

He needs just four words, though, to sum up his main message, one that should not be repeated at the dinner table. Quarterback Dads, he says, should "chill the f**k out."

CHAPTER 3

WHAT IS A QUARTERBACK DAD?

A Quarterback Dad loves attention. Both for his son and himself.

He obsesses over height and hand size. He pushes his son to drink smoothies containing spinach. He shows videos of his son performing in 7-on-7 drills to strangers. He questions the credentials of his son's offensive coordinator. He not only knows his son's completion percentage, he can peg his Instagram follower count. He films every workout. He can rattle off the names of private quarterback trainers from every region of the country. He lurks during Zoom calls between his son and quarterback tutor. When he speaks of "branding," he is not referring to cattle.

A Quarterback Dad is the football equivalent of a stage mom.

The characteristics?

"Overbearing," says Allen Trieu, the Midwest recruiting analyst for 247Sports who receives both texts and bribes from fathers hoping for a favorable rating. "Quarterback Dads have their hands in everything their child does. They watch every rep, talk to every person involved. Advocating for their son is great, but they're over the top. They think their kid is the best. They make the kid work out a lot and they want people to see that.

"I feel bad villainizing them because they really love their son. They care about him. But they cannot see the flaws."

Marv Marinovich was the world's first celebrated (and demonized) Quarterback Dad. He wore the label with pride. In 1988 Sports Illustrated's Doug Looney wrote a piece under the headline: "Bred To Be A Superstar."

Those who read it will never forget it. As summed up three decades later in a 2019 SI piece by Michael Rosenberg: "America's first test-tube athlete, they called Todd. The Robo QB. Marv stretched his son's hamstrings at one month old and had him teething on frozen kidney and trying to lift medicine balls before he could walk. Marv used Eastern Bloc training methods and consulted as many as 13 experts, including biochemists and psychologists, to build his quarterback."

Marv, who played at USC and briefly in the NFL before becoming a strength and conditioning coach, called himself "a tyrant" and bragged that his son "has never eaten a Big Mac or an Oreo or a Ding Dong."

One time, according to Esquire, Todd got a bloody nose during a Pop Warner game. Marv persuaded the coach to put his son back under center, his nose still bleeding. Todd eventually starred at USC and started for the Raiders. But he burned out after drugs overtook his body and overshadowed his talent.

Donovan Dooley has diagnosed 15 types of Quarterback Dads — 12 problematic, three good. He puts more than 80% in the first grouping:

1. **The Reminiscer.** This dad is still talking about the tackle he broke to win a JV game in 1997: "Back in my day …"

2. **The Braggin' Dad.** He believes his son has never overthrown a receiver. The kid was too short.

3. **The Not-In-Touch-With-Reality Dad.** He's the one sending Dooley clips of his son's *flag* football game and proclaiming: "There's no quarterback in the country who can do what my kid can do. He is top tier. Tons of private trainers want to work with my son, but we choose you."

4. **The "We" Dad.** He can recite the stats of every quarterback on the roster. He knows the opponents well enough to project wins and losses before the season. He considers himself part of the team, saying: "This is how many yards we threw for." And regarding his son's high school or college selection: "We haven't made our decision yet."

5. **The Over-The-Top Dad.** He films everything — games, drills, workouts. Sometimes with the aid of a drone. After the workout, he wonders: How many coaches should we send this film to? "The answer," Dooley half-jokes, "is absolutely none."

6. **The Jealous Dad.** After attending a workout, he asks Dooley: "Who was the other kid? How many offers does he have?" The Jealous Dad not only believes the other kid is overrated, he scours the internet for negative material. At camps he ignores his son's own misfires while recording the other kid's bad throws. He might even send the video to a college coach with the text: "*This* is who you're recruiting?!"

7. **The Helicopter Dad.** He's the one who peppers his son with questions on the way to a workout: "Got your towel? Got the ball? Both balls? Got your cleats? You need to perform well. We didn't drive all this way for you not to perform."

8. **The Demonstrator Dad.** This dad responds to Dooley's instruction by interjecting: "Coach, I've been telling him this since he was 5 years old." Then he forces his son to agree: "Haven't I? Haven't I?"

9. **The Really-Not-In-Touch-With-Reality Dad.** The one who approaches his son after a workout and says: "You were spinning it out there, buddy. You were lighting it up!" This is also the dad who, after hearing that another player won MVP at a camp, walks off and mutters: "This is just a money grab."

10. **The Dad Whose Kid Has Real Potential.** He stands off to the side and doesn't speak to anyone. He wants other dads to approach him with plaudits for him and his loins.

11. **The Stat-Hungry Dad.** He coaches his son, engineering the offense and game plan to give him the best possible chance to throw for 3,000 yards. Why? So recruiters will notice. His son doesn't have ideal size, so he hopes gaudy stats will make up for it. He is fine sacrificing potential wins for stats. The other parents can see it.

12. **The Gym Rat Dad.** As father and son approach a camp registration table, the dad barks: "Roll up your sleeves! Show your arms! Did you put lotion on them? That's what these coaches want to see!" The dad can recite the son's lifting maxes down to the half-pound. He doesn't realize that top quarterback prospects rarely touch the bar at the NFL combine. Guess how many times Josh Allen benched 225 pounds? N/A, not available. Allen merely performed the agility drills.

The flip side:

1. **The Helpful Dad.** Before training sessions, he asks Dooley: "You guys need anything? Water? If you want me to film, Coach, let me know." He fist-bumps his son after the workout ends, and they head off for froyo or ice cream.

2. **The Hands-Off Dad.** He wants Dooley to keep it real and shoot him straight, asking: "Can my kid play?" He sits in a folding chair at workouts and observes. He chats with other parents. He's friendly. As Dooley puts it: "He is the parent you want. I call it normal. Unfortunately most Quarterback Dads ain't normal."

3. **The Coach Dad.** He's a current high school or college coach who understands what is best for his son. He sits at the top of the bleachers during training sessions, keeping quiet and show-

ing no emotion. He might train his son at home, but he lets Dooley run the show at workouts.

Pep Hamilton is an example. The quarterbacks coach and passing game coordinator for the Houston Texans has been training college and pro quarterbacks since 1997, when he transitioned from actual quarterback to quarterbacks coach for Howard University.

He groomed Andrew Luck both at Stanford and for the Indianapolis Colts, with Luck telling reporters: "I love Pep … heck of a coach, heck of a guy."

In 2020 Hamilton helped first-round pick Justin Herbert transform from L.A. Chargers backup to NFL Offensive Rookie of the Year. So, yeah, he knows his stuff. And as a dad, he knows when to back off.

Son Jackson is a freshman at Pearland (Texas) High School who already has offers from Maryland and Texas A&M. But Dooley and Steve Wilson are his primary trainers, with Dooley saying of Pep: "He lets me do my thing. He wants to stay in that 'dad' role. He has a great perspective."

Hamilton jokes that Jackson is his "lab rat" but advises Quarterback Dads: "There comes a time where you have to take off the Quarterback Dads hat and be willing to listen and evaluate the emotional state of your kid. Don't allow the pressure and high expectations to discourage him."

Jackson is a charming, mature kid with an air of sophistication. While in Arizona for the training sessions with Kurt Warner and Dooley's crew, he ordered Eggs Benedict. He embraces his father's role in the game and has sat in on countless meetings.

"He has been treating me like an NFL quarterback," Jackson says, "since I was 8 years old."

CHAPTER 4

THE RELUCTANT QUARTERBACK DAD

Google "Quarterback Dad," and his is the first name you see. Talk to coaches who deal with obsessive Quarterback Dads, and his is the first name you hear.

Todd Marinovich. He is the living embodiment of what happens when a father touches his wife's tummy and decides what comes out will be a star quarterback. And nothing will deviate from that plan.

Marv Marinovich did not permit his bride to ingest salt or sugar during her pregnancy. He didn't allow Todd to eat a Big Mac or Ding Dong. The truth is, Todd actually did. But he was too scared of his abusive, bullying father to acknowledge it.

Marv revealed his tactics in the seminal 1988 Sports Illustrated piece titled: "Bred To Be A Superstar."

Those old enough to have read it will recall the paragraph labeling Todd "America's first test-tube athlete," one who was ordered to do push-ups before he could walk and carried his own healthy birthday cake into parties.

Marv enlisted various experts — biochemists and psychologists in addition to trainers and experts in throwing mechanics — in his quest to transform Todd, a naturally laid-back SoCal kid, into the Ultimate Quarterbacking Machine.

"I actually wanted to play receiver," Todd says now. "Catch a couple of passes, go get pizza and then play some video games. But that was not the plan, and I didn't dare open my mouth."

Todd survived the experience. Barely. How many times has he been in prison? How many times in rehab? I didn't want to ask and dredge up the past, and the numbers don't actually matter.

What matters to Todd is helping to raise his preteen children, Baron and Coco. They split time with him and his ex-wife's parents.

One of the keys to being a good parent, Todd jokes, "is to be a good referee. I didn't sign up for this."

He also didn't sign up to become a Quarterback Dad. It just happened. Baron, you see, loves football. He wants to play tackle, like some of his friends. Todd will not allow that, not until Baron is a high school freshman and has watched a two-hour documentary called "The United States of Football."

Todd is friends with the creator, writer/director Sean Pamphilon. The film details Pamphilon's quest to collect the information he needs to decide whether to allow his son to play tackle football.

"It changed my whole perception," Todd says. "I was so naïve in my thinking. We should put out an APB that says: ALL THE MOTHERS WERE RIGHT. The kids who said, 'My mom won't let me play' … they intuitively knew."

Once the Obedient Quarterback Son, a lefty flamethrower who dreamed of wearing Super Bowl rings, Todd is now the Reluctant Quarterback Dad, wary of head trauma.

Only recently has he obliged Baron's requests for quarterbacking help. The two worked together on footwork, with Todd feeding his son a classic dad line: "Fundamentals are like vegetables. They're great for you, but you're not gonna like 'em."

In terms of release point and all that, Todd says: "I haven't taught him anything. He just throws it. And he would rather play wide receiver. But looking at his skill set, if he wants to play, I hate to say it, (quarterback) is the position."

Is Todd conflicted?

"Absolutely," he says. "It is brutal."

Todd lost the power to make decisions in his life on July 4, 1969. That's the day he was born.

Marv did permit Todd to play basketball, and Todd loved competing against the likes of future UCLA Hall of Famer Don MacLean. But Marv also made Todd transfer high schools and forced him to participate in track, namely the 440-yard dash.

"Who would choose to run that?" Todd says "It's painful. That's as far a distance as a human being should sprint."

Todd attempted to steer Baron into baseball. No surprise, Baron is a natural on the mound. But he doesn't enjoy it. He loves flag football and craves to add the helmet and shoulder pads.

What's Todd to do? Give his son the independence he never enjoyed? Or protect him from a game he believes inflicts "brain damage" on some of its participants?

"My dad didn't let me make the decisions, and people saw the writing on the wall before they saw the wall," he says. "With Baron I am going to let him make the decisions. But I might have to step in — and I fear that. I believe the job, if it is a job, of parenting is to protect your kids when you see danger. And I see a lot of danger.

"I do want him to be involved in a team. A team is *so* important; I don't care what it is. But I don't see him bowing out from football unless I take that option away. I don't have to make that decision today, thank God."

Todd is nothing if not introspective. And earnest. He's still not the most dependable. Calls and texts sometimes go unanswered. He's trying.

Todd spent a great deal of time with Sports Illustrated's Michael Rosenberg in 2018, and the result was a brilliant, lengthy piece titled: "Learning To Be A Human Again."

The story opens: "His name is a parenting epithet. Overcoach your kid, get too excited about a touchdown or a home run or a goal, and you might hear it, even in jest: You're just like Marv Marinovich! Look at Marv Marinovich over here! The story is part of American lore, the ultimate in Sports Dad Goes Overboard."

You'll see references to the story in this book.

Archie Manning read the 1988 SI piece as a 38-year-old father of three and recalled thinking: "Let's not go down that path. We wouldn't have anyway, but it made me ultraconscious."

Pat Fitzgerald read it as a 13-year-old and says he associates Marv Marinovich with Earl Woods, who also nurtured a superstar athlete prone to addiction and erratic behavior.

"With a guy like Tiger I'd argue it worked out great, though not perfect," says Fitzgerald, the highly respected Northwestern coach. "And Todd did get to the highest level."

Todd broke Orange County high school records and became national player of the year. He guided USC to a 1990 Rose Bowl win over Michigan and made the All-Pac-10 team as a redshirt freshman. The Raiders, though, failed to see the writing on the wall, selecting Marinovich 24th overall despite his feuds with the Trojans coaching staff and an arrest for cocaine possession.

Todd was gone from the NFL after two seasons, eight touchdown passes and nine picks.

Barely five years earlier, Marv had remarked to SI writer Doug Looney: "Todd has the background, heredity, environment and opportunity. I just don't think he can fail. His limiting factors are the blocking, the receivers and the ability of his coaches."

If that is not the perfect reflection of the mentality of some Quarterback Dads, what is? My son has everything. He can do no wrong. If only his coaches and teammates don't screw him up ...

By any objective measure, Marv was a nightmare of a father. It's one thing to prevent your son from drinking a Coke. That's not a crime. Assault is. In the SI piece that ran in January 2019, Todd says Marv struck him with an open hand after what he deemed were poor performances in games or practices. He also assaulted people at Todd's football, basketball and baseball games and once threw Todd's mother onto a dining room table.

"A raging beast," Todd told Rosenberg.

But not without some upside as a molder of athletes, Todd said during our hourlong conversation.

Marv assembled a dream team of trainers and experts, even enlisting legendary college baseball coach Augie Garrido to help with Todd's pitching. Marv's obsession with diet and training regimens, Todd says, "gave me a huge advantage. And it gave me a lot of confidence because I sure as hell didn't believe in myself. I'm still full of doubt. Without his unwavering belief in my ability, I don't think I would have entered the arena."

Most summer days, Todd points out, were not exactly torture. He and Marv would go to the beach to train. Once the training was complete, Todd was free to spend time with friends — an effective motivation tool.

And the crack of dawn was for roosters, not Todd.

"He let me sleep," Todd says. "Nobody was to mess with me. That was one of his greatest rules: Don't wake him up; he is growing. I milked that till I was 18!"

Todd says that during high school there were moments he considered quitting football, but "the train had left the station and I felt there was no way I could stop it. I felt the toughest years were behind me."

Todd began smoking pot in high school to cope with his anxiety. In an even greater act of rebellion — wink, wink — he sometimes ate Mickey D's and other junk food. He even worked up the nerve to eat the Halloween candy he collected.

"As much as my diet was scrutinized, I'm a believer that all those years of eating fantastic set the stage for me physically," he says. "And I've come full circle. I choose to eat the way my dad made me eat because I love the way it makes me feel. The Whole Foods salad bar, are you kidding me? I used to run from the beets. Now I run to them."

So you might be wondering: How does the Reluctant Quarterback Dad handle what enters Baron's body?

Marinovich also has an internal conflict on that, saying: "Am I doing what's convenient or doing what's right? I wish I could say I'm doing what's right every time, but that is not the truth."

Short answer: Yes, Baron is allowed to eat dessert.

And, yes, Baron is allowed to eat fast food. Well, with a giant asterisk.

"There's only one place I take him," Todd says. "It's In-N-Out (Burger)."

The man has standards.

CHAPTER 5

THE ULTIMATE QUARTERBACK DAD

The Ultimate Quarterback Dad would never call himself that. Archie Manning, you see, is not one to brag.

Sure, he sired Peyton and Eli Manning, two of the greatest ever to throw a spiral. They combined for four Super Bowl titles, three Super Bowl MVP awards, 18 Pro Bowls, two retired SEC jerseys, 11,020 NFL completions and records for the most touchdown passes in a season (55, Peyton) and the longest touchdown pass in a game (99 yards, Eli). And they crushed it during those alternate Monday Night Football "Manningcasts" by casually mixing humor with heaps of knowledge.

But even hearing someone else brag on one of his boys has been known to raise Archie's ire.

Decades ago during a game at Isidore Newman School, a friend observed Peyton firing darts and remarked to Archie: "He's going to be a college star."

Archie shot back: "You don't know that; you're not a college scout. You're not a coach. How do you know that? Be quiet."

So you can imagine how the low-key Archie feels about the modern Quarterback Dad, the one likening his son to Steph Curry in shoulder pads.

Recently Archie noticed grandson Arch on a list of the top 10 players in Louisiana. (Arch is, in fact, rated as the nation's No. 1 player in the Class of 2023.)

"It was name, school, position, weight/height and Twitter (handle)," Archie says. "And Arch Manning was the only one without a Twitter account. That made me grin."

Arch's father is Cooper Manning, Archie's oldest son.

"I'm proud of the way Cooper is going about it," Archie says.

There is an interesting twist here, a commonality Archie has with modern-day Quarterback Dads. Archie didn't merely attend his sons' games. He videotaped nearly every play, resting a camera on his right shoulder from his perch at the top of the stands.

But his aim was different. He didn't seek to generate publicity. His sons, thanks to their talent and last name, didn't need any to draw attention from college scouts.

Peyton was named Newman's starting quarterback as a sophomore. Cooper was his top receiver. By videotaping the game from a wide angle, Archie could record what Peyton, Cooper and the other 20 players did on every snap.

Archie did not actually purchase the recording equipment. As the Saints' standout quarterback, he did endorsement work for an Oldsmobile dealership in New Orleans. He also helped train young salespeople through recorded role-playing exercises.

"The dealer bought a big-time, very expensive video camera," Archie says, "The lens was two feet long and you'd put the VHS tape right in it. He figured I'd want one, so he bought one for me. I thought: What am I gonna do with this? I started taking it to the games.

"I'd have a big strap over my shoulder. I looked like Channel 2 showing up! But then I could go home, slide the tape right into the VHS and watch the game."

Archie enjoyed rewatching the games and encouraged his sons to study film with their coaches.

Why? Because he did not want them to become human battering rams. Archie played in the NFL from 1971-84 and got sacked 396 times, which ranks 19th in league history. Some defensive linemen, such as Jack Youngblood, were known to ease up on him out of sympathy. Or, perhaps, humanity.

According to Lars Anderson's book "The Mannings," Archie offered this piece of advice to Peyton before his sophomore season at Newman: "You've got to know what you're doing out there because then you can get rid of the ball. And when you get rid of the ball, you don't get hit."

In other words, identify the most likely open receiver before the ball is snapped.

Sage advice. But it was not something Archie gleaned from his own father. Buddy Manning kept it simple, espousing four rules for his son:

1. Never quit.
2. Don't talk back to the coach.
3. Never bad-mouth another player.
4. Don't "shine your ass" — a Southern colloquialism akin to not being boastful

To this day if Archie ever brags, it's likely in regard to his father.

"As far as I'm concerned," Archie says, "everything he did was perfect."

Buddy laid the foundation for Archie's work ethic and love of sports. He also set the right example with his comportment at Archie's contests, whether they be football, baseball ... anything.

Archie says his father never raised his voice during a game: "Before the game he'd be curious about who we were playing and who was pitching. Afterward there'd be a little bit of praise, never any criticism, and he would not overdo it. Supportive."

Archie Manning, born in 1949, was raised in Drew, Miss., and one time his Little League team lost to a squad from nearby Marigold. Archie struck out to end the game and cried as he walked to the car.

"He did what a dad should do," Archie recalls of Buddy. "He said some words of support and mentioned how good the pitcher was. Plus he said: 'Be a man. You'll get 'em next time.'"

Buddy was 5-foot-7 but played guard on the gridiron. He was "country tough," as they say, and never backed down. Archie read in Buddy's senior yearbook that if a brawl ever started, his dad would be in the middle of it.

Buddy managed a farm machinery store, selling, leasing and servicing Case tractors. He spent long hours on the job, cognizant that his community needed him. Oftentimes he'd tell Archie that he would not be able to make his baseball game on a weekday afternoon.

"He wasn't always there," Archie says, "but he was there more than he said he'd be. I'd look up at 4:15 and see him. And he was proud. Don't think for a minute that if I had a good game, he wasn't."

But he never went overboard. No ass shining. He made a point of expressing as much enthusiasm for daughter Pam's activities.

"Me winning a Friday night football game was no bigger deal than her being in a class play," Archie says.

Buddy and Archie would sit together in the family living room to watch St. Louis Cardinals games and listen to Ole Miss football. Archie collected bubble gum cards and dreamed of becoming the next Johnny Unitas, Bobby Layne, Y.A. Tittle or Charlie Conerly. Always a quarterback.

He began playing football in sixth grade. His Pee Wee coach allowed him to call his own plays.

His skill level grew faster than his frame. He weighed 135 pounds as a high school sophomore and suffered a broken left arm as a junior. But he stuck with it; he didn't quit.

He became an Ole Miss legend, married college sweetheart Olivia and began raising boys: Cooper, then Peyton, then Eli. They all learned to mimic their daddy's five- and seven-step drops and competed in pass-catching competitions as Archie chucked passes from the porch.

The ultimate lesson from the ultimate Quarterback Dad, though, centered on four sweet words that have nothing to do with football: Be a nice guy.

That sentiment came directly from Buddy.

In 1978 Archie was named NFL Man of the Year. He referred to his father in his acceptance speech: "He told me I should always remember that it was important to be a nice guy, whether I turned out to be a great football player or not."

Cooper was the cut-up, a natural entertainer who bore a striking resemblance to Peyton. On nights before Tennessee football games, fans would see Cooper out at a bar, mistake him for his brother and ask: Hey, shouldn't you be getting ready for the game?

Cooper would reply with something along the lines of: Hey, we're playing Kentucky. What's the big deal?

Eli, meanwhile, was the quiet one. He said nary a word for years and barely participated in his own college recruitment.

The nice guy test came with Peyton, who smoldered with competitiveness and intensity no matter the sport.

During Little League baseball practices, Peyton would boss around his teammates, demanding they take extra cuts in the cage or infield practice. Archie would tell him: "Hey, everybody is not like you. Some kids just want to show up."

One time after Peyton's youth football team lost, the volunteer coach admonished the players, saying: "The reason you lost was that you didn't have your minds ready to play."

Peyton shot back: "The reason we lost is that you don't know what you're doing."

Archie made Peyton go to the man's house to apologize.

As Buddy always told Archie: The coach is in charge.

Archie generally shied away from being the head coach of his sons' teams, but one time he was put in charge of Peyton's youth basketball team. He drafted players based on whether he knew their parents, leaving Peyton as his only skilled player.

"Why did you draft these guys?" Peyton barked. "What's wrong with you?"

At Newman, tackle football began in sixth grade. At least it did for Cooper. The school changed it to seventh grade while Peyton was in elementary school. A concerned Archie asked Oliva: "You don't think he's gonna burn the school down, do you?"

The head coach of his sons' youth teams often asked Archie to serve as an assistant. If time afforded, he always said yes.

But Archie would stay clear of his sons. He'd opt for mission impossible, helping the least coordinated kids so they'd feel better about themselves and perhaps be able to contribute. If you could so much as attempt to dribble a basketball, the starting quarterback of the New Orleans Saints was here to help.

In football, Archie would offer to coach the receivers. That would help Peyton and Eli indirectly.

"I'll get a couple of 35- or 40-year-old guys come up to me in New Orleans and say: 'Mr. Manning, you coached me when I was 10,'" Archie says. "That's a kick to me. Makes me proud."

Archie is forever linked to New Orleans and the Saints. The team was abysmal in the '70s, best known for 2-11-1 seasons (in both '72 and '74) and leaving some bored fans to watch games through holed-out paper bags. In 1975 he was sacked an NFL-record 53 times.

But Archie hung in the pocket for 10 seasons, giving New Orleans his prime years. He made the Pro Bowl in 1978 and '79 for non-playoff teams. In 1981, the Saints rewarded him with a benching.

Just as Archie never griped about his porous offensive line, he took the proper tone at home: "This has been especially hard on my boys. We have man-to-man talks at bedtime. They ask why I'm not playing and I tell them everybody ought to sit on the bench for a while. We become better people through struggles."

Management shipped him to the Houston Oilers in 1982, but it wasn't so bad.

Archie rented an apartment in Houston and would hustle to the airport after practice and jump on a Southwest flight to get home in time for dinner. He'd return on the last flight out at 10:30.

Sometimes Archie would take his boys to Houston and, during practice, ask the team's third-string quarterback to babysit them. Future Quarterback Dad Oliver Luck always said yes.

After Archie got traded again, to the Minnesota Vikings, he made a special effort to bond with 3-year-old Eli, who was remarkably shy. They'd go on long walks around the lake.

Archie retired after the 1984 season when his boys were 11, 9 and 4. The family had a meeting to discuss their next move with the thought of relocating to Mississippi, the home state of Archie and Olivia.

But the boys liked their schools and wanted to stay put in New Orleans. So the family did.

Archie settled in as a sports dad and, eventually, a Quarterback Dad. He'd notice loud-mouthed parents using video cameras to record their sons' exploits and once remarked to his wife: "If they ever turned that camera on themselves, they would not be proud."

Even when he was no longer a member of the Saints, he felt he represented them in public. So while other parents chirped about ball-strike calls from an umpire making a few bucks a game, Archie strived to be a saint.

Before games, Archie's advice to his boys would not center on hot routes or blitz protection. It was something we should all tell our kids before sending them onto the field: "Remember to always have fun."

LESSONS

Appreciate the journey: For 25 years, Archie and his boys have met in Thibodaux, La., for a four-day camp called the Manning Passing Academy. Archie is executive director and Peyton, Eli and Cooper are senior associate directors.

The Mannings teach what they call 5 Pillars of Strength: To be physically strong (aerobic conditioning), mentally strong (positive habits and behaviors), emotionally strong (internal fortitude and adaptability), spiritually strong (life of purpose) and fundamentally strong (skill development for quarterbacks, receivers, running backs and tight ends).

More than 1,000 kids typically attend. Archie will zoom around in his golf cart, overseeing the operation and chatting with parents.

"Everyone thinks their son is going to be the next Joe Montana," he says. "That's fine; that's good. But I always just say: Football is like a yo-yo. It's up and down. Appreciate the journey!"

Don't be an obsessive dad: The 1988 Sports Illustrated piece on the Marinovich family ("Bred To Be A Superstar") impacted everyone who read it. Archie recalls his reaction: "That was a good lesson to me: Let's not go down that path. We wouldn't have anyway, but it made me ultraconscious."

At the behest of father Marv, Todd Marinovich went through his childhood without eating fast food. He used only homemade ketchup.

Archie observed this obsession up close. He recalls attending a Quarterback Club banquet in Washington, D.C., with Sonny Jurgensen. The wait staff served everyone a filet with potato and a vegetable. Almost everyone. Todd Marinovich, who was being honored, received two plates of fruit. Sonny turned to Archie and said: "Can you believe this?"

Back at the hotel that night, Archie and Sonny noticed a teenager staggering in after having had too many. It was Todd. He might have been passing on Coke and Sprite … but not all detrimental drinks.

"Look, I don't want to put that family down," Archie says. "But at the end of the day, that's not the right path. In their defense, as a dad with three sons who played sports, I understand how you *want* to be involved. You love your child and want what's best for him. But I think there is a right way to handle that."

Don't rush into tackle football: Archie recommends flag football until perhaps seventh grade.

"It's the best," he says, "especially for the skill positions. No tackling or equipment. Kids learn to catch passes, cover people, follow a designed play. They learn the team concept, how to win and take a loss.

"Why do third- and fourth-graders need to have all that equipment and be tackling each other? Usually there's one kid bigger and faster than everybody else and they pitch the ball to him and nobody can tackle him. I had a friend coaching a team and he asked me to stop by. I said: 'That's the offense? Hmmm ...'"

Resist the urge to interfere: Although Archie collected hours of footage of his sons, he used it far more for entertainment than instruction. If one of his sons asked for a breakdown, Archie was careful not to say anything that might contradict their coach: "I was always conscious of interfering, so I stayed out of the way."

He sometimes brought home NFL film but less so as the boys got older. He did not want to isolate himself in a dark room; he preferred to help them with their homework. So he'd get his work done at the complex and shift into dad mode under the family roof.

He would not organize workouts for his sons. But they never had to ask him twice to participate: "When they asked, I'd go. But I never said: 'Get the gloves' or 'Get the football.' They were going to have to instigate that."

Allow them to choose their college: Ole Miss not only retired Archie's No. 18 jersey, it made 18 the speed limit on campus. So when Peyton flourished into a high school All-American, many Rebels fans simply assumed he would choose to wear the red and blue. Big brother

Cooper had done just that until having to medically retire from football.

But Peyton also looked at Florida, Florida State, Notre Dame and Texas, among others, and formed an unbreakable bond with David Cutcliffe, the offensive coordinator at Tennessee. Head coach Phillip Fulmer did not try to encroach on that relationship, nor did Archie.

"I love Ole Miss, but I love my son more," Archie said famously. "I want him to go where he'll be happy."

Peyton actually gave his parents an opportunity to overrule his decision.

"Don't even think about it, son," Archie said. "It's your life, not ours."

Looking back now, Archie recalls this: "There were Ole Miss people — certain Ole Miss people, not all of them — who thought I should make that decision for Peyton. 'That's your job as a parent to deliver Peyton to Ole Miss.'

"That's ridiculous. Peyton loved Ole Miss, but things weren't great there and he made a terrific decision. Five years later Eli kind of bailed me out, but it wasn't my influence at all."

Indeed. Eli chose Ole Miss. On his own. Both decisions set the foundation for iconic careers. And no resentment toward their parents.

Know your role: Many teenagers need their parents to serve as a human alarm clock. Not Peyton. He was so self-motivated, so driven, so obsessed with watching film, Archie once told him: "You need to get out more. Get a girlfriend. Go to a movie."

Now Arch is slinging it at Isidore Newman, the school his famous uncles attended. Recruiting interest is such that coaches Nick Saban and Kirby Smart, whose teams dueled in the 2022 national championship game, appeared at the school in January to watch him play *basketball*.

Archie wasn't permitted to attend many games in the fall of 2020 because of COVID-19 restrictions. Sometimes he watched from the other side of the fence. Other times the amateur videographer caught the streaming edition of the game.

"I'm just a grandaddy," he says. "I don't get too involved."

CHAPTER 6

'I NEED YOU TO FIRE ME'

Donovan Dooley's football journey began at age 6. It was not love at first sight. On his first play, he whiffed on a tackle.

"When it was cold, I wanted to sit in my parents' car," he says. "And when it was hot, I wanted to take my pads off."

At 7, he joined the East Side Falcons and developed a love for the game when he learned that X's and O's were not merely letters of the alphabet. He obsessed over schemes and formations, poring over pamphlets of plays. He watched film of youth games on VHS tapes. In church he'd design plays in a notebook instead of reading the Bible. He learned the hand signals used by Florida State's Charlie Ward, a Heisman Trophy winner.

Dooley was more into baseball and basketball when he was little, but older brother William (nicknamed "Bug" because he was "into every damn thing") noticed Donovan's arm and steered him into foot-ball. At 8, Dooley was running the triple option and emulating one of his heroes, Nebraska's Tommie Frazier. He and William chose the team name to honor Deion Sanders. Prime Time.

His father, William Sr., didn't know much about football. But that didn't stop him. He'd shout advice from the sidelines, prompting Donovan to wave him off.

"Don't do that," William Sr. would bark, "or I'll come on the field."

33

"Hey," Donovan would reply, "let the coach coach."

Donovan would complain about it to his mother, Ella. She says William Sr. was "very tough on him" during games. And Donovan resented it.

"When I say he hated it, he *hated* it," she says.

Dooley continued to study the game and developed into the starter at St. Martin de Porres, an all-Black Catholic high school in Detroit that produced NFL players Alan Ball and Rodney Culver. Dooley led the Eagles to the Division 7 state title in 2001.

After Ella was diagnosed with breast cancer, Dooley considered it a death sentence and stayed home for college. She didn't ask him to do that. She was the kind of patient who refused to cry in front of her kids so as not to worry them. And she'd take off her wig, displaying her bald head proudly to proclaim: I will be OK.

Dooley chose Division II Wayne State in Detroit but encountered a losing culture, reflected in the team's first game in 2002 — a 34-0 stomping by Northern Iowa.

With Ella in remission, his parents suggested he transfer. Dooley landed at El Camino College, a community college in Torrance, Calif. There he met his kindred spirit, a man named Ron Jenkins.

"The most knowledgeable man I'd ever heard in my life," Dooley says.

Jenkins, who played at Fresno State, taught him the craft of quarterbacking — the intricacies of footwork, timing, progressions, protection and reading coverages. Under Jenkins, who coached the El Camino quarterbacks, Dooley learned the West Coast offense by watching 49ers film: "He gave me the keys, the answers. He skyrocketed my love of X's and O's. I brought that back to the city."

He also learned more about selflessness. Jenkins encouraged Dooley to leave El Camino because the starting quarterback was the head coach's son, a code he could not crack.

Dooley transferred to West Los Angeles College and received an education unrelated to academics — or football. His kitchenless apartment off Crenshaw Boulevard was so small, he and roommate Jareko Taylor shared a bed. But not in the traditional sense. They alternated nights, with the other sleeping on the floor.

Meanwhile Dooley learned about what he called "West Coast life."

In hometown Detroit, rival factions carved out their turf. There were lines, real and imagined, that people did not cross. Think Eminem's "8 Mile."

In L.A., the clothes speak. Hats and colors carry gang affiliations. Purple signified the Grape Street Watts Crips. The Hoover gang wore orange, often an Astros hat with a capital H. A gang in Long Beach wore blue and gold. A red Phillies hat was also not to be worn. Or one of his hometown DET hats.

Dooley went to Slauson Swap Meet, a superstore near Western Avenue, and loaded up on white Pro Club T-shirts and gray jogging shorts so "people would leave me the hell alone."

He heard gang calls and saw people flash signs during games. He even had to worry about how his mother dressed when she went to his games.

But Dooley got what he came for — a conference title under coach Darryl Holmes and scholarship offers from D2 schools. He chose Michigan Tech sight unseen, and that was not the wisest move.

The school had nothing in common with Detroit except for the "MI" in the mailing address. Michigan Tech is located in the state's Upper Peninsula, 550 miles from Detroit. The student body was lily white and most of the football players were Packers fans, as Green Bay was 200 miles south.

Dooley faced such an intense blizzard on campus move-in day, he had to literally slide down to his residence. He was ineligible until Week 4 because some of his class credits were not accepted. But once he got the chance, he started and was named player of the game against Saginaw Valley.

His father refused to fly, and Dooley now had a son, Donovan Jr., in Kalamazoo. He supported him by taking the nastiest job imaginable — security detail at Zug Island, an industrial dumping ground outside Detroit loaded with abandoned cars, feral cats and rats. He made $10 an hour, and the offseason work left him with black soot under his fingernails.

He longed to get closer to both his father and son. So he wrote a letter to Craig Rundle, the head coach at Albion College, and reintroduced himself. Albion is a private liberal arts school in the center of the state, roughly halfway between Kalamazoo and Detroit. Its coaches recruited Dooley out of high school, but he did not want to play Division III ball.

Now it would be perfect: a winning program, a respected coach, a family atmosphere, a terrific degree — and a financial aid package to ease the burden. He thrived there and stayed on after graduation as a coach, mentoring quarterbacks and successfully recruiting African Americans. He pushed school officials to give minorities coming from underprivileged areas a chance. Detroit native Chris Greenwood thrived so much as a cornerback at Albion, the Lions drafted him in the fifth round and he spent parts of four seasons in the NFL.

Dooley rose through the ranks to become quarterbacks coach and offensive coordinator at Albion and loved his assignment. But D3 assistant coaching jobs are about as lucrative as mining for gold on the beach. So he left to become athletic director and dean of students at Flint Center Academy, a charter school no longer in existence. The job provided stability, if not stimulation.

After about 18 months, Dooley approached Ron Newton, the school's principal, and said: "Hey, man, I need you to fire me."

What?

"Listen, I have this vision," he explained. "It will be called Quarterback University. I have to live my passion."

Newton's reply: I can't fire you. You haven't done anything wrong.

"I need you to fire me. Say you're downsizing or something. I need the unemployment."

It was the summer of 2011. Dooley was 26 and, coincidentally, received 26 weeks of unemployment while he researched the quarterback training industry by scouring the internet. He wondered: Who is doing what I'm trying to do?

At first he charged just $30 an hour and did his training at Oak Park High School, near the Detroit Zoo. People running on the track noticed him working day and night. But even at their pace, the joggers made faster progress than Dooley.

Business was so slow at the outset, Dooley winced whenever he drove past a McDonald's with his son in the car. Why? He couldn't afford to buy him a Happy Meal.

Now he can swing for steak. Dooley made his name in Detroit by harnessing the talents of Sam Johnson III and D'Wan Mathis, who both earned scholarships to Power Five programs. Now he's sought after not only in Detroit and Chicago but nationally, with parents flying him to Florida, Georgia, Colorado and California for training sessions.

Bleacher Report cited him as a top-10 "quarterback guru," and his pupils have started games for Big Ten and SEC schools. He trains more than 200 prospects and it easily could be more.

"Now," he says, "I'm turning down kids."

CHAPTER 7

'HE IS DIFFERENT'

Trae Taylor emerges from his family's 2017 Chevy Traverse with a radiant smile and cute little freckle on the bridge of his nose. A Mini-Me of Patrick Mahomes, Taylor is wearing a black hoodie emblazoned with these words: "NOBODY CARES; WORK HARDER."

Trae's work began at 5 a.m. with a breakfast of oranges and grilled chicken. He weight-trained for an hour, took a 45-minute break, downed a smoothie and then began his conditioning. Some days he does yoga with an instructor; others he completes footwork drills or mimics the throwing motion with towel whips.

He does all this under the supervision of his father and coach, J.R. Taylor, who scored 51 touchdowns as a running back at Eastern Illinois.

J.R. had to be talked into getting married and having kids. Here's how he recalls the moment wife Hilary's water broke: "She went into labor in the middle of my fantasy league draft."

The reluctant father is now the quintessential Quarterback Dad, transporting Trae to camps in locales such as Las Vegas and Canton, Ohio, and recording his throwing sessions — with a camera affixed to a drone.

Trae has more than 8,000 combined Twitter and Instagram followers, and if that doesn't seem all that outlandish for a 13-year-old, this will: He designed his own logo for "branding" purposes, J.R. says. It also served as a fun family project during the pandemic.

Trae's website (qb-t3.com) is sleek and loaded with photos, information on upcoming events and archived highlights from both football and hoops. It's both a digital scrapbook and an ode to the three words now enriching some college athletes: name, image and likeness.

"Trae is the golden child with the All-American story," Donovan Dooley says. "Black dad, white mom, nice kid. Speaks well, gets excellent grades. He is the pretty-looking horse, a youth phenom."

J.R. is a junior, and Trae is actually Phil Winston Taylor III. So the logo has a prominent "3" that interlocks with a "T" inside a triangle that represents "energy being funneled in," the family says.

Dooley believes Taylor is a future pro, citing a combination of mechanics, intelligence, length (tall parents) and desire. "Different" is the word Dooley uses.

Asked if the 5 a.m. wakeups are over the top for a prepubescent kid, Dooley replies: "Is it too much? Yeah, at times. But if the kid is dialed in and wants to do it ... you'd rather have a kid be active than lazy."

Dooley knows other dads who think J.R. is too demanding of Trae. Sometimes Dooley chides J.R., saying: "Hey, man, he's your baby."

"Nah, he's gonna get it," J.R. shoots back.

Meet Trae, and it's hard to be critical of anything J.R. and Hilary do. He is delightful. And polished.

Asked about his football aspirations, Trae replies: "First is to make it to a big-time college and start at quarterback. My next one is to make it to the NFL and start, but I'd be OK with not starting my first year. Because Patrick Mahomes and some other guys didn't originally start because they needed to learn the playbook and get the feel of the atmosphere."

I ask him: Do you remember whom Mahomes backed up in Kansas City?

"Alex Smith."

Nailed it.

"My next one," Trae says of his aspirations, "would be to make it to the Hall of Fame."

Asked to list his favorite all-time quarterbacks, Trae offers this:

1. Joe Montana
2. Tom Brady
3. Drew Brees
4. Troy Aikman
5. Patrick Mahomes
6. Lamar Jackson
7. Randall Cunningham
8. Steve Young
9. Tony Romo (J.R.'s teammate at Eastern Illinois)
10. John Elway

"What happened to Warren Moon?" J.R. asks.

"Oh, yeah, he's No. 1," Trae replies. "I'll take Elway out."

Trae did a class project on Moon, explaining: "I needed someone that made a change in the world. I chose a Black quarterback and needed someone that had an issue getting through his life. I looked up Randall Cunningham, but it didn't really show as much information.

"So I did Warren Moon, and it showed how his dad died and he started (his career) in Canada. He would bake cookies before every game. It relaxed him. He had six sisters. That must not be good for anybody. They would stress him out and he'd make cookies."

I mention to the family that I have a connection to Moon through his California-based agency, Sports1Marketing. I get Moon on the phone and tell him about his not-so-secret admirer.

His response?

"First, I'd tell him I love the fact that he used me as an example for his stories. But why did you look up Randall Cunningham first?" Moon says with a chuckle. "I don't like being second fiddle to anybody.

"Tell Trae I said good luck. Whether he's going to be a quarterback, a businessman or a doctor, it will take hard work. The more work you put in, the more you will get out of it. More so for me at the time because of my skin color, I knew I'd have to be that much better to make it. And then once I made it, I had to work harder than the other guys."

Trae is an only child. The family's eggs reside in his basket.

J.R. grew up a Cowboys fan and had the talent and size (6-2, 215) to play in the Big Ten. But after an issue arose with his ACT, only the coaches at Eastern Illinois stuck with him. He became a Division I-AA (now FCS) All-American, rushed for 241 yards in a 2001 game against Southeast Missouri and helped lead the Panthers to three straight playoff berths.

"Definitely the right choice," he says. "If I had gone to a big school, I wasn't going to class. There, they made sure I did."

The Packers signed him as an undrafted free agent, but Taylor could not crack a running backs room that featured Ahman Green, Najeh Davenport, Tony Fisher and fullback William Henderson.

He played for the Montreal Alouettes in the CFL and then a handful of semipro teams in the Midwest — the Peoria Pirates and Roughriders, the Chicago Slaughter, the Milwaukee Bonecrushers, the Rockford Raptors and the Racine Raiders.

He made it in football, you could say, but he never made it big.

Dooley says having a father who played is "never a minus because he understands the grind of the game — and some of the recruiting."

And if you think that means college recruiting, you're only partially right. Trae, a seventh-grader at Bernotas Middle School in Crystal Lake, Ill., is being sought after by numerous high schools in Chicago's northern suburbs.

The rules seem convoluted. High school coaches are not allowed to contact the Taylor family, so they use go-betweens who are not actually employed by the school — typically a program's volunteer coach.

J.R. is a volunteer coach at Crystal Lake South, Trae's local school. The plan is for Trae to go to either Crystal Lake South or Carmel Catholic in Mundelein, about 30 minutes away. The head coach at Carmel is Jason McKie, a former Chicago Bears fullback.

"We can reach out as much as we want," J.R. says. "He can't even respond on a text chain."

Asked what he's looking for in a school, Trae starts: "It's based on the football program ..."

J.R. cuts him off, saying: "That's not what it is."

Trae continues: "... *and* the academic side. I don't really know the academic side of Carmel Catholic; I've only seen the football. I'm looking for a program that can help me evolve."

Evolve. What a heady kid.

Asked if it's important for him to start as a freshman, Trae replies: "I'd like to. But if all they want me to do is play JV, I'd be fine with that."

Crystal Lake South has a solid but unspectacular program that rarely sends players to Power Five schools. One enormous exception: The 6-foot-6, 324-pound Trevor Keegan, who chose Michigan over the likes of Georgia and Ohio State in 2019. He now starts at left guard for the Wolverines.

"Our coaches are nice men," J.R. says, "and good with kids."

The family won't overcomplicate the high school decision. More complicated, potentially, will be Trae's college choice. A half-dozen schools already have inquired through Dooley, including Michigan State, Penn State, Michigan and Tennessee.

"In the end, Trae will be able to close his eyes and point to a school," Dooley says.

"He is athletic, he can sling it and he has the arm talent. He has all the intangibles ... and these long-ass arms!"

J.R. and Hilary married in 2006 after a courtship that began at Eastern Illinois. A one-time competitive swimmer, Hilary met him while working as an athletic trainer for the football team.

"I told her: I don't want to get married. And I don't want to have kids," he says with a chuckle.

Says Hilary: "I was like: 'Yeah, right, OK.' We had a niece who pulled at his heartstrings."

With Hilary on the cusp of delivering, J.R. did the right thing. He dropped her off at Advocate Sherman Hospital in Elgin, Ill., and then finished drafting his fantasy team. She delivered Trae by C-section on Sept. 2, 2008, and it was a struggle. He had a lung infection and spent several days in intensive care.

"A rough start," Hilary recalls.

Trae came home wearing Cowboys gear, and his crib contained several stuffed footballs. He began throwing competently at age 4 and snuck onto a flag football team with older kids.

His father began coaching his team, the Lake in the Hills Junior Eagles, when Trae was 5.

"He wanted to play running back because that's what I played," J.R. says. "I said absolutely not. I did not want him taking all the hits from these older, bigger kids. And understanding how my body feels now ... I'm not doing that to him.

"I said receiver or quarterback, and he picked receiver. I was fine with it. I didn't want people to think: He's starting at quarterback because his dad is the coach."

But then ...

"Our quarterback took a hit and decided to quit in the middle of the game," Trae says. "So I went and played quarterback for the rest of the game, and I didn't switch."

Here's why.

"I scored on the first play," Trae says. "The play was 'regular fake 24 boot left.' I was supposed to keep it on the rollout, and I did. I had two stiff-arms and made one kid miss and I scored. It was like 60 yards."

Says J.R.: "That's weird that he remembers that play. I just saw the video of it."

Trae: "It was versus Gary (Indiana)."

J.R.: "Yeah, it was."

I ask Trae if he has a freakish memory for football.

"Yeah, I can tell you that Barry Sanders and Calvin Johnson never played in a Super Bowl," he says.

And then he turns to Dooley, who is from Detroit.

"Sorry," he says.

Pretty good awareness for a preteen.

It provided a glimpse of things to come.

CHAPTER 8

TICKETS AT WILL CALL

As Trae Taylor loosens up before a throwing session in the fall of 2020, Donovan Dooley warns: "We're gonna treat this like a pro day. You ain't gonna get too many warmups. Four more and then you're ready to rock 'n' roll."

Trae and five of his Pop Warner teammates have gathered at a park across from a Catholic church in Winnetka, Ill., on Chicago's North Shore. There are no swings or seesaws. The 40-yard field not only has a pro-caliber FieldTurf surface, it has white lines marking every five yards.

The location fits. These players are here to work.

Dooley will run the throwing session while three other adults observe. Trae's mother, Hilary, stands nearby, arms folded. Mike Hohensee, a private quarterback trainer and former pro, watches intently. J.R. Taylor, Trae's father, sets up the recording equipment.

Soon enough, a drone will buzz overhead, recording video that will appear on Trae's social media accounts in the form of a two-minute package.

Is the drone too much?

"For that kid and this group, that's OK," Hohensee replies. "These guys are serious about ball, serious about fun and serious about each other. They'll have cameras on them."

Dooley agrees, saying of J.R.: "He's excited. His son is being interviewed. He wants to show that this is part of his son's journey. Everything is documented. God willing, Trae will have a story to tell."

The story is unfolding in real time. The first chapters have been written.

Allen Trieu covers Midwest football recruiting for 247Sports. He is one of the most identifiable names in the industry, writing weekly columns for the Detroit News and appearing every National Signing Day on the Big Ten Network. At camps, he often draws more attention than the prospects.

He recalls attending a camp outside Chicago run by Pylon 7on7 Football. Organizers gave him a start time, but when he arrived, Trieu noticed only smaller kids working out. He considered leaving to get a bite to eat.

"The scout in me said: Stand here and watch for a minute," he says. "So I do. And after three throws, I point to a kid and say: 'Who the hell is that?'"

Trae Taylor, he was informed. You haven't heard of him?

"No," Trieu told those gathered around him. "I don't go digging around middle schools."

At the throwing session in Winnetka, Trae is wearing a short-sleeve red athletic shirt with a hoodie. Compared with the quarterbacks who play on Sundays, Trae's right arm is as slender as the shaft of a golf club. But he uses it to unleash rockets that could dislocate a thumb.

Trust me. I caught a few from 10 yards away and then waved him off, quitting before I risked a visit to the emergency room.

"Look at his balance," Hohensee says. "He's always centered. He's not falling off. A lot of the high school kids will stumble as they throw, almost like a drunk coming out of a bar."

Hohensee chuckles. He began coaching quarterbacks in 1990, primarily in the Arena Football League. He was the first head coach of the Arena League's Chicago Rush. He played in Canada and the USFL, served as a replacement player for the Chicago Bears during the 1987 NFL strike and threw the first touchdown pass in Arena League history. He has seen some things, mentored his share of gunslingers and game managers.

Being around Trae makes him giddy. The two began working together when Trae was 8.

"With quarterbacks," Hohensee says, "I talk about how they're being judged from the time they walk out their front door in the morning until they get home at night — judged by the bus driver, the lady handing out lunch, every teammate, the coaches in other sports. Why should he be our quarterback? So you have to prove yourself every single day.

"Trae's one of those kids who eats it up. He wants all of that. He wants to be the guy everyone's judging. That's why I think he's going to be a great leader in life. He's going to be so much more than a great quarterback."

Hohensee is so bullish on Trae's future, he says his big reward will be watching Trae play on Sundays from a stadium suite.

He jokes with Trae: "Just leave me some tickets at will call. I'm willing to pay for tickets to watch you ... but don't make me."

And similar to what Earl Woods predicted for his son Tiger, who is also biracial, Hohensee declares: "Trae will be so much more than a great quarterback. I think he will be a great leader. Think about what's going on with race relations and everything. That kid, that kid will be ... it."

At this moment Trae is following instructions from Dooley, who says to the group: "We'll do slants, hitches, digs, skinny posts. Front side and back side. And then I'm going to have Trae call plays that you guys should know."

Trae lines up in a shotgun formation. There's no defense, only a center and receivers.

"Ready!" he barks. "Go!"

He fires a strike to a receiver on an out pattern. Then he takes a three-step drop and connects on a crossing route.

"He explores everything," Hohensee says. "Watch what he does with his eyes. He ain't eyeballing the receiver; he's manipulating the safety. He is keeping his shoulders open so he can read the defenses."

A few plays later, the 5-foot-7, 120-pound Taylor rolls right and throws over the middle. The pass is complete, but Trae smacks his hands together, frustrated. The pass was maybe six inches behind the receiver. In a game, it might have prevented him from gaining yards after the catch.

"He loves football for a lot of the reasons everyone loves football," Hohensee says. "But he also loves it because it challenges his mind and his body. He was chosen for it too. Some kids don't want the mental part. He wants it all. He wants the ball in his hand. He wants the chalk in his hand."

"Ready … go!"

Trae fires high to his 5-foot receiver.

"My bad," he says.

"Little more air," Hohensee comments.

While Hohensee stresses mechanics, Dooley focuses on what he calls "the cerebral … understanding coverages and fronts, eye discipline."

To that end, Dooley's favorite part of the throwing session is about to begin. Dooley will bark out situations, down and distance, defensive coverages. Trae will decide what to run.

"It's on you," Dooley tells him.

Trae fires high and wide of a receiver who ran an unexpected route.

"Ooh, miscommunication right there," Dooley says to Trae. "That's on you."

Trae talks to his receiver to clear things up.

"Fix it," Dooley tells him. "You have to sort it out."

Next play, Dooley tells Trae to select the "hot" receiver who has been preselected to counter a blitz.

Trae goes under center.

"Hot, hot," he calls out. "Ready ... go!"

He takes a two-step drop and quickly hits the slot receiver.

Hohensee says of the decision to go under center: "Smart move. Why risk a bad snap when you can hit a home run?"

Dooley ends the session by setting up a scenario: "OK, listen. You must get a first down to win the game. It's third-and-9. It's '3 sky' and they are rolling strong."

Trae makes a call — "Spartan Hawkeye!" — but there's confusion.

"Delay of game," Dooley says. "Now it's third-and-14. Let's go."

Trae looks left and fires right. The pass is complete on a slant route.

Dooley tells him good job and puts out his fist for a bump. The two barely connect because Trae is looking downfield, telling a receiver: "Make sure you're between the linebackers."

Is he America's youngest player-coach?

He certainly has the memory for it.

"The first year we played," he says, "we lost two games. The first was to Buffalo Grove and the entire middle of the field was muddy. Second time, we lost in the playoffs. Got our butts kicked by Prairie Ridge, like 34-0.

"We haven't lost a Super Bowl since. I'm not losing again like that."

Other times, Trae sounds like a kid. Asked which Big Ten schools interest him, his first response was Clemson.

He also said his favorite subjects in school are "P.E. and art because she (the teacher) doesn't have us do anything."

But the first line in Trae's Twitter bio (@Qb6Trae) is "GPA: 4.0" and his family is serious enough about academics to require a minimum result of 80% on every test.

Trae says he once got a "79.9%" on a pop quiz and had to sit out the first half of a game. J.R. actually recommended a full-game benching, but Hilary said half was enough.

"Trae was totally fine," J.R. says. "No complaining, no moping."

Says Trae: "I wasn't going to be a sore loser about it because I did it to myself. Plus I knew the (opposing) team sucked, so ..."

Chuckles all around.

J.R. coaches his son's teams, but he leaves the quarterback tutoring to the specialists.

"I see dads' and kids' relationships, and I don't want it to be a fight all the time," he says. "For me, being a Quarterback Dad is understanding that even though I have more of a grasp of football than most, I don't know (everything about the position). Instead of me calling the plays, Trae does it. It helps that he is self-driven."

He knows it looks a little odd to film so many training sessions. For games he flies a drone-controlled camera for wide-angle shots and pays a cameraman $80 to focus his lens on Trae and the offensive line.

"We watch film," Trae says. "Last year there could have been a mistake and we wouldn't see it."

J.R. began posting clips of Trae on social media when he was 7. But it was more occasional, and the feed also contained basketball and taekwondo clips.

"Originally I was not filming everything, and then I met some very important people (at a camp) in Georgia," J.R. says. "This father pulled me aside and said: 'Trae is amazing. How come we didn't know about him?' I said: 'Because he's in the third grade and we live in Chicago. Why would you expect to know him?'

"He went on to explain to me about some running back named Billy. I said: 'What does this have to do with me and Trae?'

"He said: 'It's a circuit, and you need to get your kid on social media so people know who he is when he's coming in from other states.'"

That argument did not win over J.R.

But this did: The reason Trae got invited to a 2018 camp at the Pro Football Hall of Fame in Ohio was that someone forwarded Facebook clips to the organizer. And that led to an amazing experience, with Trae posing alongside jerseys of Aaron Rodgers and Joe Montana.

"If you ask Coach Dooley, (players) are starting to get scholarship offers in seventh and eighth grade. That's how crazy it is. Should we wait?"

J.R. ponders this briefly.

"Or should we get out in front and get him all the best opportunities?"

CHAPTER 9

THE LOW-KEY QUARTERBACK DAD

The word "freak" gets tossed around a lot in college football these days. Bruce Feldman of The Athletic and Fox Sports composes an annual "Freaks List" that ranks the college game's sickest athletes, guys who can outrun Tyreek Hill and bench-press Patrick Mahomes' Ferrari.

Peyton Ramsey is a different kind of freak. He has played quarterback since he was old enough to grip a football. He starred in high school, appeared in 32 games at Indiana and led Northwestern to the Big Ten West championship in 2020. And yet Ramsey has never worked with a quarterback trainer. No gurus, no sages, no swamis.

He has received coaching from, well, his coaches.

"Very, very unusual," Ramsey says about his decision to go solo. "I don't think I've met another quarterback in college who did not have his own trainer or at least someone who he works with when he's back home. I just never felt the need."

That simple, down-home view reflects Ramsey's upbringing in football. And the low-key nature of Doug Ramsey, his Quarterback Dad.

Doug is one of the most respected coaches in the Midwest. He has won more than 200 games at Cincinnati's Elder High School, where he became head coach in 1997.

He was an acclaimed quarterback in his day, good enough to earn a scholarship to Louisville, where he played one season.

Asked about his own quarterback training, Doug replies: "Nothing. Back then you played football, basketball, baseball in the spring and more baseball in the summer. And I wouldn't take back any of that. I got to do the things I loved. The vast majority of kids I coach in football play at least one other sport."

He sounds as proud of that fact as he is of the Division I state titles Elder won in 2002 and 2003.

Doug and Cherie Ramsey have four kids, including three boys who excelled on the gridiron. They were all named for quarterbacks: Tanner (i.e. Montana, for the legendary 49ers signal-caller), Peyton (you can guess) and Drew (for Bledsoe).

Tanner switched to fullback because of his frame — 5-9 and 220 pounds when he played at Elder.

Drew is a slot receiver and wildcat quarterback fielding offers from MAC schools. He scored four touchdowns in his father's 200th victory, a 55-48 playoff win over Colerain in 2021.

Only Peyton, the middle son, stuck with quarterback. But that sentence does not reflect Peyton's wide range of athletic interests. It does reflect the No. 1 piece of advice from the Ramseys: Do not specialize.

"Especially at 12 years old," Doug says. "I truly believe guys get better when they wrestle and play basketball and run track. Baseball, think of the mental part. There's a runner at third with two out and you have to get him in. I think those (mental challenges) are more beneficial. If you specialize, I don't think you will be as good as you can."

Doug reminds people of when Peyton received his scholarship offer from Indiana. It came after Hoosiers offensive coordinator Kevin Johns observed him competing against city power Archbishop Moeller — on the basketball court.

"It was not just his athleticism," Doug says, "it was the way he carried himself on the court."

Peyton played basketball all four years of high school and says:

"If I was good enough to play baseball, I would have done that as well. You learn the competitive piece from playing other sports. Plus if you're playing only one sport, you might burn yourself out. When all you're doing is footwork drills in the backyard … I think that's scary for young kids to focus heavily on one sport."

Tony Pike has emerged as the top quarterback trainer in Cincinnati, parlaying his strong college career with the Bearcats and brief time with the Carolina Panthers into a training career. Although Pike is a family friend to the Ramseys, Peyton never worked with him.

"Just never really felt the need to change my mechanics," Peyton says. "I'm not saying there aren't awesome quarterback guys out there, but some might hurt you more than they help you. I worked hard in the weight room and grew up in a football household with my dad around."

Doug is the antithesis of the classic Quarterback Dad, worthy of his own made-up adjective: underbearing.

"I was pretty hands off," he says. "Very hands off."

He did coach his sons, but in basketball. And Little League baseball. That was partially a function of his job — his Elder players take top priority from August to early December. On Thursdays, Doug would end practice relatively early, by 5 p.m., and then hustle to watch his sons practice.

And we do mean watch. He stood and observed, silently.

"He'd never say anything," Peyton recalls. "It was really good for our (father-son) dynamic. We had this unwritten rule: We would not talk about the good and bad (of football) during the car ride home or at the dinner table. We'd talk about family things."

Doug put Peyton in the hands of his youth coach, Brian McKeown, who helped linebacker Luke Kuechly develop into a seven-time Pro Bowler.

"I let him do his thing," Doug says. "I wasn't critical, and at the same time, I was never overboard with praise: Oh, you're so great. My wife did a great job with that too. We don't brag; we just want you to play hard and good things will happen."

Doug finally began coaching Peyton during his sophomore year at Elder. And that brought some scrutiny.

Elder had a returning quarterback in senior captain Nick Peters. Doug used the first two games as an extended tryout and felt Peyton outplayed Peters a bit. Not everyone agreed.

As Doug told Cincinnati sportswriter John Fay in 2015: "There were doubters. No one said anything (directly) to me. But people would come up to me and say so-and-so said he can't believe your son is playing.

"The thing is, (Peyton) is really good. He's the hardest-working guy we've got. He doesn't lose sprints. Every rep in practice is meaningful to him. … It would be hard if your son was kind of a dog."

Elder has what you'd call a passionate fan base. Cherie typically watches games from the visitor's side at the home field, called The Pit. Doug jokes that in his early years, as a result of attending games, his sons thought his first name was "Dumbass."

Elder has a Tuesday Night Dads Club held in the school cafeteria. Fay, an Elder grad, described it this way: "Dads drink beer, watch film of the last game and loudly question play-calling. Mind you, that team won a state championship. I was amazed Doug subjected himself to it."

In his typical understated style, Doug says it's not that bad: "The doors open at 7 and then at 8 I'll come in and show the previous game film. It's not really breaking things down, it's more like: Hey, here's who made the tackle, watch this lineman make a block. It's a way to point out some positive plays."

The dads use it as a fundraising vehicle to support the team. Doug is grateful for the ones who make and serve sandwiches at summer practices during two-a-days.

Doug uses it to remind the dads not to be critical if their sons don't appear on the stat sheet. Maybe young Jimmy took on a blocker that allowed a teammate to bring down a running back.

"Dads, don't tell your kid he has to make a tackle," Doug says. "Tell him to do what he is coached to do."

And of the criticism at the events, Doug says: "It was really hard when I was young. Now I'm a gray-haired old man, so I don't hear nearly as much."

Neither Ramsey is a fan of outside noise. They favor honest evaluations from those inside a small circle of trust.

"Some parents are not realistic with themselves and think their kid is the greatest quarterback on the planet," Peyton says. "Be truthful with your kids."

Doug has an understandable bias toward high school coaches. If a parent is interested in hiring a personal quarterback tutor, he recommends the parents first ask his son's coach: Is there someone you know and trust?

Above all else, play multiple sports. And don't apply pressure. Be underbearing.

"Don't push your son out of the game," Doug says. "It's got to be fun."

CHAPTER 10

'LEBRON JAMES OF FOOTBALL'

Jay Underwood was a classic Quarterback Dad. In every maddening sense.

His mood depended on how son Bryce performed in a workout. He rejected professional coaching because he deemed all the trainers unworthy of his son's talent. He viewed Bryce as a prized possession, gazing his way and thinking: I made that.

On the ride home from practices, Jay would grill Bryce: "What's the problem? Why did you half-ass it?!"

If Bryce tried to ignore him, Jay would bark: "Oh, no, we're gonna talk about it!"

Bryce would retreat to his bedroom and slam the door, while Jay would remark to his wife: "He's *your* son. And he's trippin'."

Jay now understands the damage he caused — or nearly caused.

"He was 10," Jay says, "and I watched him suffer. I knew he was a great kid and football player, but I was trying to control him. I coached him and pushed him, and his response got worse and worse. Now I'm not coaching him and the relationship is amazing."

The Quarterback Dad now strives to be a Dad Dad.

Jay mainly leaves the coaching to the professionals — his son's coaches at Belleville (Mich.) High School and Donovan Dooley, who gushes about Bryce: "If he is not the No. 1 quarterback in the country (for his age), he is definitely in the top five. He is athletic, long, hard-working, a grinder. He has it all — the moxie, the confidence, the arm talent, the length, the demeanor, the hunger. You would think he is 18."

At the time, he was 13.

"Man, he's gonna be special," Dooley says. "Recruiting for him will skyrocket."

Dooley said that in September 2020. Four months later, I spoke to Bryce for the first time. He declined to mention the news of the day: Kentucky had offered him a scholarship, his first.

"I don't even know how to celebrate," he said.

It is borderline indescribable. An SEC school offered Bryce a full ride before he attempted a pass in high school — and seven months before his 14th birthday. Next came an offer from a Big Ten behemoth: Michigan State. In June, Michigan. Bryce celebrated that by tweeting out pictures of himself in head-to-toe Wolverines gear, including a helmet. Then Tennessee followed.

Bryce is also not what you'd call loquacious. Asked to describe himself as a quarterback, he replied: "Dual threat."

That's it?

"That's it," he said.

Kyle Short, the offensive coordinator and quarterbacks coach at Belleville, was not surprised to hear about the brevity.

"When I listen to him do interviews, he is an introvert," Short says. "He does not express himself. But he is a goofball, fun to be around. We have a lot of fun together, especially on the field. And I've never met someone who has to have a football in his hand and wants to throw it all the time."

Bryce might not have the gift of gab in public settings. But he has ability. And hunger.

"Other 14-year-olds are playing video games. He is going to Planet Fitness or LA Fitness to work out," his father says. "Or he's calling Donnie to bug him about coverages. He is trying to stay two steps ahead. With his size (6-foot-2, 190), the way he plays, how he carries himself and his confidence, you gotta see him."

Asked how far his son can take football, Jay pauses and replies: "I believe he can be an NFL player, absolutely. To me he can be the LeBron James of football."

Whoa.

Underwood did not play on a team as an eighth-grader. The family played it COVID-safe. And yet as a freshman, Underwood beat out the competition at Belleville to start the opener — plus every game after that.

Belleville reached the Division 1 playoffs and advanced to the state semifinals, where Underwood fired three touchdown passes and ran for a fourth. Detroit's Ford Field hosted the state title game, and what Lions quarterback Jared Goff wouldn't give for these numbers: 284 passing yards, five TD throws and 64 rushing yards with a score.

Underwood rallied his team from a 17-7 deficit to beat Rochester Adams 55-33 for Belleville's first state title. Detroit Free Press sportswriter Mick McCabe saluted Underwood for "literally (tearing) up Ford Field with an amazing individual performance" and opened his column by listing Underwood's birthday: Aug. 19, 2007.

His point: Underwood did all this less than four months past his 14th birthday.

"Once he becomes a senior," Belleville receiver Jeremiah Caldwell said, "it will be mind-blowing."

Short interrupted one of Underwood's postgame interviews to tell him: "You grew up before my eyes."

He is not the only one who continues to evolve.

Jay still has a tough time letting go. The reformed Quarterback Dad came up with the perfect analogy: He is the driver's ed instructor in a car with two steering wheels. Bryce is gripping the one on the driver's side. But Jay cannot put his hands to the side.

"I can't let it go," Jay acknowledges. "I've tried my best."

Case in point: Jay allowed Bryce to select Belleville, even though the father was angling to move the family to Houston. But about a month before the season, Jay attended a practice. He felt it was so disorganized, he sounded the alarm.

Short replied: "It's a month before the season and you're telling me you might have Bryce go somewhere else? I just moved here. I'm coming to build structure and discipline. Give me some time, at least one season."

Jay then opted to join the staff as a volunteer assistant. He says it was logical given that Belleville's head coach, Jermain Crowell, also coached him in high school. Asked if that was a condition of Bryce choosing Belleville, Jay talked around it.

"I tried my best *not* to be on the staff, to stay in the stands and just watch the program evolve," he says. "But the program was so behind, I had to get involved. I came with my ideas. (Crowell) said: I need you on the staff."

Jay says that when he "stepped on the field, the coaches all looked at me like: He is coming out here just to protect his son. Which was absolutely true! But I'm also striving to be a great motivator and mentor and to push the kids to see how far they can go."

Jay not only has more self-awareness than most in his shoes. By all accounts, he did a terrific job with the Belleville receivers. Short said he was "stern and demanding. But I didn't think we'd get to the point where he would be on the sideline for games."

Yup, the Dad Dad morphed into a Quarterback Dad on game days.

And the problem there occurs between offensive series. Instead of huddling with Short, Bryce's first instinct is to look for his father.

"I'll say: Where is my quarterback? Where is 19?' I see Jay is right there with him," Short says. "One of Bryce's deficiencies is that sometimes he gets low after an interception or sack. I have not found the magic key to get him out of that. One time I was talking to Bryce one-on-one in the middle of a game, and Jay came up and pulled him away. He said: 'I'm his Dad. I have that right.'"

Says Jay: "When he is down, I will pick him up and get out of the way. I don't want to be a distraction. I quickly remove myself."

How does he pick him up?

"I ask him: What are you feeling out there? How can we make it right? I give words of encouragement," Jay says. "I don't raise my voice. I'm past that. I take the dad part away and act as a friend, help him out.

"Kyle and I bumped heads a few times, and we may continue to do so. He is the offensive coordinator and he wants to build that relationship with Bryce. What he doesn't understand is that's my son! I gave him some pointers to build that relationship, and toward the end of the season, it was phenomenal. I saw them laughing and joking, having a good time on the sideline. That translated to the field. The game became that much easier for Bryce."

The relationship between Jay and Short, who also works with Dooley at Quarterback University, reached a high point on the night of a playoff game. After the Belleville victory, Short checked his phone and noticed a lengthy text that arrived 14 minutes before kickoff.

Jay had messaged him: "Have a great game … I'm definitely impressed with the growth … I've always been on my son's sideline to make sure he is good. I'm slowly making an exit to make sure I can be a fan of my son. Please don't be afraid to push him to his limits. I built him for this."

That game, Jay watched from the stands. Kyle figured that would become the new norm. Well … not so fast.

Turns out Jay's decision was based on timing: He worked late at FedEx and could not arrive until warmups. He didn't have time to change into Belleville gear and didn't feel right joining the sideline. He watched from the stands and said he enjoyed the view.

But after the game, he says, special teams coach Calvin Norman noticed him in street clothes and said: "That you, J-Wood? Don't let that happen again. We need you down here!"

Says Short: "He wants to be in the stands. But something pulls him to the sidelines and prevents him from truly handing those reins over to me."

Bryce comes from great stock. His mom, Beverly, is 5-11. She's not an athlete but her brothers are boxers. Jay played free safety and tight end in high school. Asked if he was any good, Jay replies: "Oh, I was great! But not as good as my son is right now."

Jay wanted to pursue college football, but his parents needed support. So he went to work at the post office and later Comcast.

"They were not really into supporting my dreams," he says, "so I'm trying to make sure my son can cross the finish line, no matter what."

Jay was seriously injured when Bryce was 5. A driver knocked him off his bicycle, and the accident was so serious, Jay said he had to learn how to read, walk and talk again. He was in the hospital for weeks and did months of rehab. Bryce became his de facto coach.

"Just like I taught him to take his first steps, he was right there with me, pushing me, motivating me," Jay says. "Our bond is crazy. At that time, I told him: I will do whatever it takes to get you to where you want to be."

Jay thought that meant being hands on. Ten fingers. At all times.

Bryce began playing football around his seventh birthday. Because he was big for his age, coaches suggested he play on the line. Jay would have none of that, saying: "We shopped around until we found a team."

Jay coached him that first season for the Motor City Bears, and the team lost nearly every game. Bryce wept but insisted he did not want to quit, earning his father's respect "as a fighter."

Jay had a family connection to Dooley, who began coaching Bryce at age 8. But Detroit's most highly acclaimed quarterback tutor was not good enough. So Jay, who never played quarterback, took over. The results were a disaster.

"I coached him and I pushed him, and his response got worse and worse," Jay says. "I was probably one of the worst dads out there. And his attitude sucked. I was trying to be his father, his coach and his mentor. I couldn't wear all three hats."

So Jay stopped listening to all the other dads who said: "Get on his tail! Push him!"

He started listening to his inner voice. And to Dooley.

"He does an amazing job," Jay says. "I love the fact that Donovan took the time to understand my son. He got behind this big monster and is not afraid to challenge him, to push his limits. Other (tutors) are scared; they fear he will walk away. Donovan knows when to raise his pom-poms and when to challenge him. And he is hard on everybody! No kid is exempt from punishment if he's laughing and joking and can't explain the coverages.

"I like how he takes his time. He's patient and gives everyone his knowledge before they do anything physical. He's a great mentor, a great coach and a great trainer."

Jay remains the father of a promising quarterback, but he says he's no longer a Quarterback Dad — at least not a harmful one. He defines that as a father who "sometimes ends up pushing his kid away from doing what he loves."

That was him a few years ago, butting heads with Bryce as he spoke of "grooming" him to become an NFL quarterback. Jay learned that didn't work for him or Bryce, so now he's on the other side, advising dads: "Do not unwrap your gift prematurely. Make sure your son sees you as a parent, not as a coach."

Great message.

And one Jay tries to remember. He jokes about one of Bryce's rewards for bringing a state title to Belleville: "My son and I made a deal. If he got to Ford Field and won, I'd step to the side, move completely out the way and be a fan."

OK, so it's settled? Games in the stands next season?

"In my heart I think I should be in the stands," he says, "but the coaches want me to stay. I know those 10 to 15 kids (receivers) need that extra motivation, so I might have to sneak out there to push them."

CHAPTER 11

'YOU CAN'T MAKE A KID PLAY FOOTBALL'

Steve Wilson mentors the quarterback mentors. He's the godfather of the personal training industry, a man equally adept at discussing Fran Tarkenton's scrambling ability, Tom Landry's shotgun-fueled passing attack and Kyler Murray's mechanics. When the makers of the Madden NFL Football series aimed to make the game more realistic, EA Sports went to Wilson.

Asked about his "Star Wars"-inspired nickname, Wilson chuckles and replies: "I don't want to be known as the Yoda. That guy was old and ugly."

More than three decades after he played in a Super Bowl for the Denver Broncos, Wilson is more of a Quarterback Grandfather than a Quarterback Dad. Having served as a father figure for hundreds of young men, the 64-year-old is still dropping knowledge on pint-sized quarterbacks and their parents, hoping to help them maximize their potential.

"I make a living by getting people to do things they don't think they can," he says of personal quarterback training.

How does he do it?

"That's for another book," he says, chuckling.

Thankfully, that book already exists. It was published in 2015 and written by Scott Stankavage, a former NFL player and Quarterback Dad whose son, Shawn, loses his way after tearing an ACL. The book documents Wilson taking Shawn, a promising quarterback in North Carolina, under his wing.

Among Wilson's countless lessons from "The QB Mentor":

- Quarterbacking is a lifestyle, and it's non-negotiable.

- Quarterbacks must seek mastery in three areas: mechanics, knowledge and mental processing.

- Learn the game and you can play at any level. It's like chess. You would never enter a chess tournament without knowing what all the pieces can do and how they work together and against each other, would you?

- The quarterback must learn the defense, and every defense has a structural weakness. He must know the defender's conflicts and exploit them.

- The quarterback is responsible for winning the game, which includes both scoring points and preventing points. Ball possession is the secret to championship football.

- 75% of plays are executed mentally pre-snap. That knowledge makes the game slower and simpler.

- You cannot win the game in the first quarter; you can only lose it.

Wilson added this big-picture gem during our chat: "You can't fool Mother Nature and you can't fool human nature. All the animals in the forest know that when (an animal) appears, they should either hunt or run. They don't need to ask a question; that is Mother Nature.

"As for human nature, you can't play quarterback worrying about making a mistake. To be great, you have to throw the ball into harm's way. You can't worry about how people perceive you ... what someone wrote in a blog or put on Twitter. We have to teach kids to deal with both success and failure."

Wilson speaks from experience. His obsession with football began at age 9 when he watched Super Bowl I, then found a brown paper bag and grabbed a crayon. He wrote down his goal of playing in the NFL's ultimate showdown.

Twenty years later, he walked onto the pristine field at the Rose Bowl in Pasadena, Calif., as a starting cornerback for the Broncos in Super Bowl XXI and asked himself: "How did I get here?"

Steve went to Howard University, where he graduated in 1979 as the school's all-time leading receiver and kick returner. Undrafted, he arrived at Cowboys rookie camp with hundreds of other hopefuls. For two days, he says, he never even got to run routes because the receiver line went in alphabetical order.

So he stayed late, running routes by himself. That caught the attention of quarterback Roger Staubach, who began throwing to him.

"He was Captain America," Wilson says, "and he saw some things in me."

So did Landry, who lost both of his starting cornerbacks to knee injuries in training camp and needed to get creative. So he approached Wilson, then a second-year wideout, and told him he'd be shifting to cornerback. After Wilson began to protest, Landry replied: Move or we'll cut you.

Wilson had never played corner in his life, and Dallas' first game was against the Redskins on "Monday Night Football." The night he learned he'd be changing positions, Wilson went home and tried back-pedaling. He fell into the street.

But Wilson had some things in his favor: He was a quick learner with a voracious appetite for knowledge. And he played every sport growing up, cross-training before it was a thing.

He survived that Monday night road game and his team won 17-3. The Cowboys limited Joe Theismann to 190 passing yards.

The move to cornerback turned out to be a blessing. It became the genesis for his second career — coaching.

"I had no edge; I had to study quarterbacks," Wilson says. "I started to understand what they could and couldn't do."

He studied all the top signal-callers of his era: Theismann, Jim Hart, Ron Jaworski, Phil Simms, Dan Fouts, Jim Plunkett and the so-called "unbreakable bond" between Jim Zorn and Steve Largent.

He joined the Broncos' "Orange Crush" defense and appeared in two Super Bowls. He lasted 10 seasons in the NFL, starting 140 games and intercepting 22 passes.

A month after he retired, he was dining at a Chili's and read in USA Today that head coach Willie Jeffries had resigned at Howard, Wilson's alma mater. He called the football offices and offered his services. Dan Reeves and Mike Ditka recommended him and he got the job. At age 31. With no coaching experience.

He coached both sides of the ball — thanks, Mr. Landry — but focused on quarterbacks and play-calling. He changed the offense from the option to a sophisticated passing attack. The Bison endured tough times, including a 10-game losing streak.

He says Howard quarterback Ted White once threw seven interceptions in a game and after the seventh, White came crying to his coach: Please get me outta here.

Wilson replied: You threw seven, but I called seven. I'm responsible too. You got me into this and only you can get me out of this!

"I gave him the freedom and authority," Wilson says. "I told him: The first thing you need to have success in high-pressure situations is courage; without courage nothing else matters."

In 1998, White threw for a school- and Mid-Eastern Athletic Conference-record 561 yards and eight touchdowns against Florida A&M. He remains the school's all-time leader in yards (9,908), completions (638) and touchdowns (92). White's final season capped a three-year run of the Bison going 24-10.

Wilson became a surrogate Quarterback Dad to numerous players, including Pep Hamilton, who says his son, Jackson, has been "born into" their quarterback dynasty.

Wilson now teaches the fundamentals of quarterback play in person to pupils in North Carolina and via Zoom to prospects such as Trae Taylor. This is a glorious time for the position, Wilson says, because of its evolution.

He loved playing with Staubach and John Elway, players he calls "mobile rocket-launchers."

But then Peyton Manning and Tom Brady entered the league, and coaches at all levels became infatuated with giant, immobile dropback passers.

"Everything was in the pocket and you had to have a real good offensive line," Wilson says. "People in college were looking for Peyton Mannings, and there were none. Even Tom Brady went in the sixth round (of the draft)."

High school coaches began experimenting with the spread offense in the late '80s and '90s, putting their best athletes at quarterback. The five-wide, no-huddle spread attack flowed to college football. Northwestern switched to it in 2000 under Randy Walker, and the Wildcats offense surged from 12.8 to 36.8 points per game.

The NFL was comically slow to adapt. One example: The Browns took Brandon Weeden, a 6-3, 230-pounder from Oklahoma State, with the 22nd pick of the 2012 draft. He ran a 4.89 40 at the combine.

Russell Wilson went 75th to the Seahawks. He's not even 5-11 but ran a 4.55. He's a Super Bowl champion and eight-time Pro Bowler.

"Kyler Murray and Baker Mayfield would never have had an opportunity were it not for Russell Wilson," says Steve Wilson, who's not related. "He knocked the door down. People now don't talk about height like they did. They're more open to the athlete playing the quarterback position."

And that's good for quarterback tutors. Coaches no longer have to project which teens will be tall. The position is open to anyone. And training is available to anyone who can afford it.

Wilson, of course, advocates for the industry, saying: "If you're a keyboard player and you can get Mozart to teach you, you take it."

Wilson has encountered every type of Quarterback Dad, half-joking: "The perfect Quarterback Dad? I haven't met that guy."

Here's his advice for fathers of promising QBs:

"The first and most important thing is to be a good dad. If you're a good dad, that's enough. The problem comes when they want to be more than good dads. There's a difference between coaching your son and fathering your son. The relationship is the most important thing.

"If you are going to coach him, it's got to be fun … fun before work! If it's fun, he will get you to work out together. If it's work, you're gonna have to get him.

"Inspire and motivate your son but don't be over the top. You can screw up his life and that is a lot to risk. I've seen guys who have moved away from their father because of that pressure.

"You cannot make a kid play football. The preparation is too hard and the physical harm is too great. When you're out practicing in the summer, it's 98 degrees; when it's time to win a championship, it's minus-3 degrees. You have to endure a lot, and kids today do not want to be uncomfortable. I would play with a frozen basketball in my backyard. You couldn't dribble it, so I'd find nine guys and we'd just pass and shoot.

"Imperfections can be a child's greatest asset. The most important thing to do is support. When your son hits adversity, get him from the darkness to the crack of light. When a child doesn't have support, they will get (attention) from elsewhere or shut down. Once they shut down, they are done.

"I've seen dads coach their sons, and it's no problem. I've also seen that dynamic destroy the whole family. Above all else, be a dad."

THE HANDS-OFF QUARTERBACK DADS

It's an unwritten rule of Quarterback Dads: The more accomplished the dad was as a player, the less crazy he will be with his son.

Take Jay Barker and Trent Green. Barker quarterbacked Alabama to the 1992 national championship, went 35-2-1 as a starter, won the Johnny Unitas Golden Arm Award in 1994 and finished fifth in Heisman Trophy voting. He's raising seven kids, including a walk-on quarterback playing for Nick Saban, in a blended family.

His parenting philosophy could best be described as hands-off. That and relentlessly positive.

"Never get into a car after a game and correct your kids," Barker says. "If they want to open up or ask your opinion, they will. Focus on the positive things — how hard they played, teamwork, sportsmanship."

Green views it much the same. His two sons blossomed into quarterbacks, while their dad started 82 consecutive NFL games.

"I didn't push football on them," Trent says. "My emphasis was to find something you like doing and do it. Just because I played doesn't mean you have to."

Barker and Green were both born in July, two years apart. Both are now successful broadcasters, with Barker hosting an ESPN Radio show in Birmingham and Green an NFL color analyst for CBS Sports.

Their fatherly philosophies have resulted in smart, respectful, high-achieving, athletic kids.

Let's learn a few things:

Their own dads set the tone: Jerome Barker, Jay says, was "amazing." He was an all-state pitcher who coached Jay in baseball and basketball.

But his love of sports was passed down through osmosis, not lectures. Jerome once told the New York Times about the time they sat on a fishing lake, and Jay remarked: "It isn't so much the will to win but the will to prepare to win."

Jay was 10 years old. Jerome chuckled and thought to himself: This kid has got it together.

Jim Green, Trent's father, was a good enough football player in high school to play at a small college. Instead, he went off to Vietnam. When Trent was 12, Jim tossed him a football and suggested he try the sport for a year.

Trent's best sport was basketball, but he gave it a shot, playing left tackle and free safety. In eighth grade, his team's starting quarterback got injured. Trent stepped in and "fell in love" with the position.

"My dad was such a patient man," Green told ESPN in a 2006 piece. "He was a salesman, then a manager, and people really enjoyed dealing with him. At his funeral, a lot of the people who attended were former customers and they seemed to have [fond] memories of him.

"I've got kind of a perfectionist personality. I'm really hard on myself. I'd be beating myself up at times and he would tell me, 'People would give a million dollars to be doing what you're doing. Do you know how lucky you are?'"

Jim Green passed away suddenly from a heart attack at age 58. At the Chiefs' first home game after the burial, Trent approached his dad's seat in Section 121 of Arrowhead Stadium and placed down this message: "Jim Green, we miss and we love him."

Barker's father also died prematurely. Jay was 22, having just completed his final NFL combine workout. He learned that Jerome had passed from a pastor/friend while at the airport ticket counter in Indianapolis.

"My dad was an encourager, not a corrector," Jay says. "And you know that episode of 'Modern Family' where Jay says 90% of fatherhood is just showing up? What's important is that your kids see you there, cheering them on."

Don't be that dad: While in high school, Green read the SI story about Todd Marinovich. He and Marinovich were in the same graduating class, going off to play college football in 1988.

"At the time I remember feeling bad about it because I felt like he was missing out on so much," Green recalls. "Football was all-consuming, and that would stink. He did end up being the top quarterback in high school and became a (first-round) pick. But he missed growing up."

Barker's modern version of the nightmare Quarterback Dad is the one who rants and raves at youth football games, making a scene.

"Do you realize what you look like? Your kid is dying inside," Barker says. "You're yelling at a ref that is making 10 to 20 bucks a game? It's so sad when kids see parents getting into fights. What is going on? This is Little League. It's not worth getting that worked up."

Barker coached his sons, quarterbacks Braxton and Harrison, through seventh grade. He allowed the parents of other players to watch practice, but he certainly didn't encourage it, telling them: "Y'all can shop. You don't have to be here."

Barker's hope for all of his players was that they would not look to the stands after a miscue. If his kids ever did that, he strove to make sure they never saw a bowed head or any expression of disappointment. Having played at college football's highest level, in the sport's toughest league, he knew all about the challenge of playing quarterback.

And once seventh grade arrived, Barker was content to hand off his sons to coaches and tell them: If you have an issue, talk to your coach first. It's his team and his time.

"The next six years," he told them, "you need to win the job. Grow up and be responsible for how you perform."

Barker's hands-off approach extended to academics.

"I'll be honest," he says. "I never even saw report cards."

He was the opposite of a snowplow parent who clears a neat path for his kid. When other parents would ask if Braxton or Harrison had completed a school project, Barker would shrug and explain: If someone turns in work late, we'll hear about it from the teacher.

"If they needed help or advice, we'd give it," Jay says. "But we never wanted to be a crutch. It worked out for us. All our kids excelled in school."

And when it came for them to select a college, Barker and wife Sara stepped aside and merely played the role of consultants.

Braxton wanted to run out of the tunnel at Bryant-Denny Stadium, so he opted to walk on at Alabama, where coach Nick Saban is to him as Bear Bryant and Gene Stallings were to their father 30 years ago.

Harrison wanted a more legitimate chance to play, so he chose Alabama-Birmingham.

That desire to work hard and excel, Barker says, must come from within.

"I just want them to know: Dad loves us no matter what," he says.

Encourage ... but don't push: Growing up, Green played everything. It was typical of his generation. When the season changed, the equipment did too: football to basketball to baseball. Or in the case of Green's wife, Julie, tennis.

So Trent and Julie encouraged their kids to do everything. He loves the fact that two of his kids take guitar lessons and a third taught himself how to play the ukulele. Perhaps that will be the companion to this book: "Ukulele Dads."

While youngest son Derek took some pleasure in Matchbox cars, big brother TJ (short for Trent Jason) had a one-track mind. He immersed himself in sports — watching and playing games and devouring ESPN's "SportsCenter."

Says TJ: "Growing up, my dad was my idol. He never really pushed anything on me; he just wanted me to be happy in whatever I did. It just so happened I loved football."

Green coached his sons in T-ball and flag football, both in the spring. In the fall he was a little busy, especially during his six-year run as the Chiefs' starting quarterback. Dick Vermeil was his coach from 2001-05, and Vermeil didn't earn his rep as a sleep-on-the-couch grinder for nothing.

Green called his schedule "severe" but said he loved playing for Vermeil, and the two remain close. Green says he took advantage of having Tuesdays off and insisted on being home for dinner and homework time every weeknight. After helping to put the kids to bed, he'd spend some time with Julie, watch tape from 10 p.m. to midnight and then rise at 6.

Vermeil sometimes let kids play in the indoor facility, so TJ and Derek would put on giant pads and throw to one another, making diving catches. TJ palled around with the likes of Larry Johnson, Tony Gonzalez, Eddie Kennison and Priest Holmes.

"Thankfully I was old enough to remember a lot of it," he says.

TJ developed into a good player at Rockhurst, a Jesuit high school in Kansas City. But he was undersized and not much of a prospect, at times asking himself: I'm Trent Green's son; how come I'm not bigger and stronger?

He passed on an offer from North Dakota State in order to walk on at Northwestern. He was set to seize the starting job in 2019 but got injured in the season opener at Stanford, suffering a broken foot that effectively ended his college career. Peyton Ramsey beat him out in 2020.

Northwestern coach Pat Fitzgerald says Trent falls in the "great" category of Quarterback Dads: "He was incredibly supportive and let

TJ learn from his experiences. He was there to guide him and help him. I can't tell you I ever talked to him about TJ starting or not starting."

Asked what comes to mind when he hears "Quarterback Dad," Trent replies: "I think it's someone who maybe was more demanding than what I was. We're throwing today! We're working on footwork, doing ladder drills, studying tape! That pops to my mind. I was always: I'm here and I'm available. Let me know when you want to do something."

It served the boys well. Derek has competed for the starting job at SMU. TJ appeared in a dozen games for Northwestern and earned multiple degrees, including a master's in data science.

TJ cautions fathers to avoid being "the annoying dad who isn't letting his kid have any free time on the weekends. As a parent you should stress that you will always be there. But don't be overbearing. Let the kid decide for himself.

"If the kid is doing it for himself, he won't burn out. Because he loves it."

CHAPTER 13

THE QUARTERBACK DAD WITH 'CLASS'

Jim McCarthy is the kind of Quarterback Dad who promises he was "quiet as a church mouse" during his son's high school games. On the ride home, father and son were more likely to talk about J.J.'s social life than his completion percentage. Even though Jim played college football, he knew when to hand off his son to the experts.

"There is a point where dads have to walk away," he says. "Unless you're Tom Brady or Drew Brees, you have to let someone else handle this. What I was teaching him was all wrong."

In the early 1990s, when Jim played running back for Division III North Park University in Chicago, coaches taught quarterbacks to bring the ball to their ear. Now it's get the proper backstroke, put the ball in a comfortable position and gain force from the ground up.

But Jim got the big lessons right. He taught J.J. to be polite and respectful, to outwork the competition and not to make excuses. Days before the 2018 Illinois Class 7A state title game, J.J. declared he would rather have his fractured thumb cut off than miss the game.

J.J. is a "yes, sir" guy in person and texts. When I arrived at his high school in the spring of 2019 to interview him for a Chicago Tribune feature, J.J. extended his right hand and said, "Hi, Coach."

The mixup was understandable. Three actual coaches appeared at Nazareth Academy that day: Texas offensive coordinator Tim Beck,

Iowa State recruiting coordinator Alex Golesh and Tennessee quarterbacks coach Chris Weinke, the 2000 Heisman Trophy winner.

At the time, McCarthy was a 16-year-old sophomore ranked No. 2 in the nation among pro-style quarterbacks in his class. Almost as impressive: his 3.97 GPA.

McCarthy visited Ann Arbor that weekend and verbally committed to Michigan, as expected. He enrolled in January 2021 and made a huge contribution as a freshman to the Wolverines, who beat Ohio State for the first time under Jim Harbaugh and won the Big Ten before losing to Georgia in a College Football Playoff semifinal. McCarthy relieved starter Cade McNamara and threw Michigan's only touchdown pass in the game.

"To have a son contributing on a college football team as a true freshman and to hear nothing but how the other players, coaches and fans love him, we could not be happier," Jim says.

It's a tremendous story, a kid from a cold-weather state defying the odds by outranking all the top pro-style quarterbacks from California, Georgia and Arizona.

And Jim deserves equal credit. He might wince when he reads that because he's not a credit hog. Or an attention hog. He is not your typical Quarterback Dad.

"When you called Jim a good Quarterback Dad, I thought: spot on," says Allen Trieu, who covers Midwest recruiting for 247Sports. "J.J.'s parents had every opportunity to ruin him. The kid gets a Power Five offer before the ninth grade and ends up with a ton more. A lot of scrutiny. Michigan does not have a good year (in 2020) and everyone is asking: 'Will he bail? Will he decommit?'

"If you could write a script on how to handle a kid's recruiting, this would be it. Jim and his wife did it with class and followed J.J.'s best interests."

The takeaways from the journey? The lessons? Read on.

Play multiple sports: J.J.'s first love was hockey, an ode to mother Megan, who figure skated competitively. In third grade, J.J. played hockey instead of football. And in later years, the family would sometimes fly to Pittsburgh or Toronto straight from a football game to have J.J. lace up the skates in tournaments.

"Hockey helped me tremendously with toughness and learning how to be a good teammate," J.J. says. "And the quickness of the game actually helped slow down football for me."

The personal time demands led J.J to make a decision at age 14 he says was his alone. Once hockey coaches suggested he needed to move to Quebec to train with top juniors, he shifted his entire focus to football and never looked back. (Though his mom cried for two weeks.)

Don't be *that* type of football dad: Jim coached J.J.'s teams for seven years and made it clear to parents what kind of behavior was acceptable. Before every season he would explain his policies. The first: You can come to practice but only if you remain off to the side.

"Do you walk into your student's classroom and tell the teachers what they're doing wrong? Or shout stuff out from hallways?" he would ask them. "I treat this area as a classroom."

Jim instituted a 24-hour rule. If a father had a gripe about his son's playing time, the dad would have to wait a day to cool off. Then he could set up a face-to-face meeting with the son present.

"So often it's not the kid who is complaining; he is smiling and having a blast," Jim says. "It's the parent questioning things."

Before games Jim would warn the parents — and more so the "chirpy" aunts, uncles and family friends — that if one of them got kicked out for harassing an official, he too would be ejected. So zip it.

And finally, to avoid having a parent come to the sideline with a water bottle, he would remind them: Our team has a trainer. If a parent needs to be present because of an injury, you will be summoned.

Jim also had a special way of responding to player complaints about a minor injury. If the player was down and hollered, "Oh, my knee," Jim would look at him earnestly and reply: "Your knee? How's your ear?!"

And often, the kid would laugh.

Know when to say when: Jim taught his son the big-picture stuff, stressing attitude and effort. And he gave J.J. no special treatment. If anything, it was the opposite.

"I was held to a higher standard," J.J. recalls. "If I ever slipped up, there were no warnings: You are running to the fence and back."

J.J. says his dad treated him like a football player, not a quarterback. That meant taking contact in practice, unlike all those college and NFL QBs who wear a red "do not touch" jersey.

"It would have been boring (otherwise)," J.J. says.

During games, Jim leaned toward letting J.J. figure things out on his own. He was given latitude with play calling, and when J.J. would turn to him with his palms up, Jim would joke: "Hey, Jesus is not gonna help you now."

Jim coached J.J.'s Westchester Raiders and Lions Football Club youth teams. But in the summer between seventh and eighth grade, he decided to branch out. He signed up J.J. for a 7-on-7 team run by Midwest BOOM Football, where the motto is: "Competition, development, exposure."

He also enlisted a private tutor, Greg Holcomb of Next Level Athletix. Holcomb is not, in Jim's words, a "hoarder" — a tutor who demands that he be the sole trainer. J.J. also has worked with Tony Ballard (Football University) in Georgia and Mike Giovando (Elev8) in Arizona.

And perhaps most important, when Jim attended the training sessions, he kept his mouth shut and observed.

"You shouldn't go to the sessions and tell your son to hold his arm up right," he says. "The kid does not want to be embarrassed because he has the wrong grip on the ball, especially in a group setting. That is why we are paying the coach!"

Chart your own course: Jim believes quarterbacks in the Midwest

THE QUARTERBACK DAD WITH 'CLASS'

start with two strikes against them because 1) the weather does not allow for year-round training and 2) reclassification, switching to a different graduating class, is frowned upon.

"In Texas and California, it's almost weird if you don't reclassify," Jim says. "If you do that in the Midwest, people look at you like you have three eyes."

Critics of J.J. on recruiting message boards pointed to his slight stature. Or make that normal stature for a budding teenager. He was 5-10, 150 pounds in eighth grade. But the McCarthy family declined to have J.J. reclassify.

That didn't deter Iowa State coach Matt Campbell from becoming the first Power Five coach to extend a scholarship — two months before J.J.'s freshman year. Nor did it keep J.J. from blossoming into a five-star recruit.

J.J. called an audible before his senior season at Nazareth. Although he loved playing for coach Tim Racki, J.J. felt hamstrung by Illinois' COVID-19 protocols. The quarantine rules were such that J.J and his workout partners got booted from practice fields during the spring of 2020. He technically was not allowed to touch a football under state guidelines, with the goal of limiting infections.

So the family decided to have him enroll at IMG Academy in Bradenton, Fla. The school calls itself home to "the world's most dedicated student-athletes."

Not only would J.J. be able to play, he would get to practice against elite competition, a unit loaded with SEC-caliber players. His top receiver, Malik McClain, signed with Florida State. A game against Duncanville (Texas) featured more than 50 future FBS players.

Iron sharpens iron, as they say.

On top of that, J.J. learned how to assimilate with teammates from varying economic backgrounds. They might have the same ambitions — a top-flight NFL career — but they sometimes described different motivations.

"He learned the difference between loving football and living it," Jim says. "For some kids, football is the ticket to help their families. In the Midwest, we love it. In SEC country, they live it. J.J. ended up being captain of the team. The guys gravitated toward him. He was a chameleon and kept everyone engaged."

J.J. says the experience of being away matured him and provided a preview of college life. It boosted his football IQ. And in terms of leadership, he continued in his quest to be his team's most dedicated player.

"It's like with Kobe," J.J. said of the late Kobe Bryant, who grew up as the son of a professional basketball player. "I come from a very blessed upbringing, and I want to show I work harder than everyone else."

Remember, everyone is watching: Father and son agree it's important to have a presence on social media.

"Stay relevant," Jim says, "but don't overdo it."

J.J. began tweeting at age 13. His background profile photo is an image of Michael Jordan clutching the Larry O'Brien Trophy. McCarthy has a following in excess of 34,000 while keeping his tweets to football and avoiding hot takes. What qualifies as his most daring tweet might be "LFG," short for "Let's F**king Go."

Says Jim, in the vein of advice: "Keep things real ... but protect yourself. Your Twitter account is your resume, your LinkedIn page. It's how coaches find you. They go through your history and can tell what you're like. Does he have a beer in his hand? As J.J. Watt put it: It takes years to build a reputation and seconds to ruin it."

(Watt's full quote: "Read each tweet about 95 times before sending it. Look at every Instagram post about 95 times before you send it. A reputation takes years and years and years to build, and it takes one press of a button to ruin. So don't let that happen to you.")

J.J. McCarthy calls social media "a sneak peek at your personality."

He is respectful but outwardly ambitious, open about his goal of blossoming into an NFL MVP. And if he's outspoken about anything, it's the topic of Quarterback Dads. He's fortunate to have a good one, and he knows it.

Asked what advice he would give overbearing dads, he replies: "Please do not yell or make faces at your kid after every ball they throw. Don't overwhelm him watching film. He's already doing it at school and maybe on his own. He does not want to be critiqued by his own dad. Don't force it on them."

Above all else, J.J. says: "Please realize that when you played the game, it was for fun."

CHAPTER 14

THE REGRETFUL QUARTERBACK DAD

Let's be honest: Unless you're one of Drew Brees' kids or a member of the Philip Rivers brood, you will not relate to the childhood described in this chapter.

"Listen," says Chris Simms, who grew up under the same roof as the MVP of Super Bowl XXI, "it was awesome. I don't know any other way to say it. For a football-crazy kid who could tell you every player's number as a 4-year-old, it was Disneyland. To wake up on a Sunday in the fall and know your dad is playing at Giants Stadium ..."

Chris, Phil Simms' oldest son, would get wheeled around in a laundry cart by cornerback Elvis Patterson. He got to pal around with linebacker Carl Banks, chit-chat with Cowboys coach Jimmy Johnson and toot the horn of Hall of Fame broadcaster John Madden's bus (aka the Madden Cruiser). He and other sons of Giants players would raid the team's gum supply and, if the mood was light, jump in the whirlpool or steam room after a victory by the G-Men.

Phil was 24 when Chris was born. So to top it all off, Chris was old enough to appreciate everything he had. But that's just a few pixels of the entire picture.

The New York tabloids could be brutal with the small-town kid from Morehead State in Kentucky. The Giants took Phil with the seventh pick in the 1979 draft, and two seasons later they went 4-12. Simms completed just 48% of his throws.

"SIMMS SUCKS" is one of the headlines Chris remembers.

Chris would sit in the Giants Stadium mezzanine with his mom and siblings during games and sometimes hear razzing. Tougher, though, was the sick feeling that came over him before the Giants faced the Eagles and their fearsome pass rushers: Reggie White, Jerome Brown and Clyde Simmons.

God, I hope my dad doesn't get hurt today, Chris would tell himself.

The Giants were the defending Super Bowl champions in 1987, and their season opener was in Chicago. The Bears mauled them, registering nine sacks.

"My dad got murdered in that game, knocked out cold, a broken hand," says Chris, now an NBC Sports analyst. "We were sitting 15 rows up and the Bears fans figured out who we were. I remember thinking: Wow, people can be this mean to a 7-year-old?"

Times have changed. We think. We hope.

They certainly have when it comes to raising and training quarterbacks. The Simms clan can tell you all about that. Phil and youngest son Matt founded a training academy in New Jersey called Simms Complete QB. Through various interactions, Phil has the Quarterback Dad stories to prove it.

He recalls the time a quarterback transferred away from state power Bergen Catholic because he wanted a chance to start. Matt called the player's father during his first game at the new school.

Matt: How's it going?

Quarterback Dad: Great!

Matt: You guys are winning?

Quarterback Dad: No, we're losing. But he's throwing it every down!

Another time, Matt worked out a preteen quarterback and the father approached afterward to ask: "So ... does he have *it*?"

Matt replied: "I don't know if I can answer that after an hour and a half."

Phil is such a strong believer in what he and his training staff espouse, he says: "If I knew then what I teach now, my whole life would have changed. ... When I was 55, I threw it better than at any time during my career. It's real. More efficient. It's about leverage, getting in the right position to really use your body."

Phil has a simple reply when parents ask him: Do you change kids' motions?

"Not if they're good."

He adds this in his twangy, G-rated vernacular: "When people say, 'You can't change a throwing motion' ... my aching rear end you can't! Tiger Woods has had about five different golf swings."

Phil developed his throwing motion on his own. That's how it was growing up in Kentucky in the '60s. Might as well have been the 1860s when it came to quarterback training.

He never touched a football in the offseason. Or lifted a weight.

His high school coach, Henderson Wilson, believed in running — in all of its various forms. Every day before football practice, Wilson made his players run a mile in full pads. On days he allowed them to do laps without helmets, the players thanked him as if he'd driven an ice cream truck onto the practice field.

Wilson was so old-school, on game days he would threaten to approach the opposing coach with a warning: We're gonna run it up the middle every bleepin' play. His actual strategy wasn't far off. As a senior, Simms did not throw a single touchdown pass until his final regular-season game.

No wonder Kentucky didn't offer him a scholarship. Or Louisville.

But it all worked out better than a bubble screen against an all-out blitz.

"I went to Morehead and played every down for four years," Simms says. "You can't beat that."

Even during college, Simms rarely lifted weights or threw in the offseason. After months of firing a baseball, he would show up for training camp, grip a football and think: Man, this feels different.

This was an era in which quarterbacks played multiple sports and didn't stress over mechanics. When Simms became a Quarterback Dad to Chris and Matt, his philosophy mirrored that. He encouraged them to play baseball and simply to give a complete effort on the gridiron.

When Chris would ask his dad about an NFL star such as Deion Sanders, Phil would reply: "I hear he's an unbelievable worker."

Phil played professionally past Chris' 13th birthday, so even if he had wanted to get heavily involved in his son's quarterback training, he couldn't have. Phil sometimes caught the end of a football practice, watching silently. Father and son engaged in serious one-on-one hoops matchups, with Phil never conceding easy buckets.

Phil actually did more coaching in basketball but limited his instructions to three words. He would stand in the top row during games, getting fed up as Chris surged past 30 points.

"PASS THE BALL!" he would scream.

"It would make the whole gym shake," Phil says with a chuckle. "The ball would come out of his hand so quick."

Phil also coached Matt's Little League baseball team, and he did it his way. He emphasized fun over winning, except during tournaments. That meant giving the green light on 3-0 counts, attempting stolen bases and protecting the arms of his pitchers. He encouraged other teams to visit because the home field had a good snack bar, and after games he threw BP to the players' dads.

Those same hands stayed mainly idle during football season. The Quarterback Dad gave his kids freedom. And now he regrets that.

"I always said: I won't be the intrusive father," Phil says. "I should have been."

Case in point: Chris' college recruitment. The USA Today National Offensive Player of the Year originally chose Tennessee but reconsidered when offensive coordinator David Cutcliffe left for Ole Miss.

Chris signed with Texas even though he knew his playing time would come at the expense of Major Applewhite, a gritty, undersized Southerner with a catchy name and penchant for comebacks. Applewhite was immensely popular after going 8-2 as a starter in 1998, the year Ricky Williams won the Heisman Trophy.

The fans and majority of students viewed Simms as Applewhite's foil — a Northerner, a Yankee, tall and gifted, the son of a two-time Pro Bowl player. They sided with the underdog, creating endless conflict.

"He could not have gone to a worse place," Phil says. "I let him go. I didn't voice my opinion strong enough. I should have been more involved. I should have been there on the visits and picked the colleges for (Chris and Matt). What 18-year-old really knows what's best for him? Hardly any. They get blinded by all the things that mean nothing in the long run.

"I tell parents: 'Make the decision and live with it.'"

Whoa. That's contrary to the advice given by most Quarterback Dads who are accomplished former players. But Phil feels strongly about it. And Chris agrees.

"He was very respectful of me making my decision," Chris says. "He still kicks himself in the butt that he let me go to Texas. And looking back, I wish he had said more. I was 18 — and f**king stupid. My dad knew the nuances of the game that I did not. If I'm fortunate enough to be in that position, I would get a little more involved."

Midway through Chris' sophomore season, Phil broached the subject of transferring. If it had been 2020, Chris would have made the peace sign and been out the door. But in 2000, transferring was uncommon. Chris was a little stubborn. He wanted to prove his doubters wrong and beat Oklahoma.

When the girlfriends of his teammates expressed concern after hearing jeers rain down from the home crowd in Austin, Chris shrugged it off. He thought about how his father had dealt with all the nasty critics.

"Dad would say things like: 'Christopher, don't worry. Most of those people don't even know what they are looking at anyway,'" Chris says. "I never knew I was good at blocking out the noise until I got to Texas. It gives me thick skin to this day. Not everyone is going to like you."

Phil and Chris now form the most prominent father-son broadcasting duo in the NFL. Phil appears on "The NFL Today" CBS pregame show and "Inside the NFL" on Paramount Plus. Chris breaks down quarterback play for a weekly segment on NBC's "Football Night in America" and examines all things football on his podcast, "Chris Simms Unbuttoned."

They live a few towns over from one another in New Jersey. They never tire of talking ball. And both are Quarterback Dads. Phillip Simms, Chris' 11-year-old son, is a Pop Warner quarterback with potential.

"He's got a chance for sure," Chris says. "He's a Simms. He has the determination, he works at it and is a good athlete. If you made me bet, I'd say he'll have a chance to be in the (recruiting) rankings."

Chris' profession affords him a bit more time to observe his son's practices. Phillip's coaches sometimes try to get Chris on the field for guidance, but this Quarterback Dad is more likely to wave them off. And like his own dad, Chris does very little with Phillip's mechanics.

"Just the basics: Get your shoulder to the target," he says. "My thing is play, enjoy it and have a ball in your hands at all times. Play three sports."

Phil fostered Chris' love of football by throwing with him in the backyard and keeping it light.

"He never, ever put pressure on me to play football or be a quarterback," Chris says. "If anything, he would rather have seen me play baseball."

And he took Chris to the Giants complex whenever it was allowed — mainly on Saturdays for walk-throughs. (As a remarkable aside, Phil says NFL teams were so tight when he played from 1979 to 1993, players were expected to bring their own lunch.) Chris would steer clear of the wisecracking Bill Parcells.

"It was not a family atmosphere," Chris says. "My dad was scared of him, so I was triple-scared. I stayed on the other side of the building."

Parcells intimidated Chris, but his father did not. And now Chris brings that accommodating spirit to his father-son relationship.

"Whenever a dad is psycho and too controlling, by the time the kid gets to the eighth grade, he doesn't want to play sports anymore," Chris says. "I had a few friends like that. Every day the kid comes out, his dad is acting like it's the Super Bowl. I'm seeing this and thinking: There's no way this kid is gonna last.

"Let him play. Of course you can guide him at times. But don't push and don't be critical. Tell him: Work hard and play because you love it."

Phil says the best Quarterback Dads are supportive. And following his own epiphany, he recommends they get heavily involved in important decisions such as selecting a college. A talented linebacker or receiver can thrive almost anywhere, with at least two or three on the field at all times. A quarterback? Not so much.

"You literally can be one of the top quarterbacks in the country and pick the wrong spot," he says.

His son did just that.

"Chris," Phil promises, "will handle it differently with his kids."

CHAPTER 15

TO BE SPECIAL, DO NOT SPECIALIZE

When he's not broadcasting games for Fox Sports or chauffeuring his three daughters around South Florida, Brady Quinn is likely to have a clicker in his hand. Not to watch "Ted Lasso." To watch film.

Quinn marvels at the divergent skills of Aaron Rodgers, Tom Brady, Russell Wilson and Patrick Mahomes. Notre Dame's single-season record holder for passing yards (3,919) and touchdown throws (39) sees a common thread.

"Tom Brady's footwork is like watching a boxer ... the way he maneuvers in the pocket and sets his feet," Quinn says. "Russell sees windows and manipulates the defense with his eyes. It seems like things are happening in slow motion. Rodgers literally jumps when he throws. With Mahomes, I guarantee he came out of the womb throwing, whether it was a Frisbee or paper airplane.

"They're all dual-sport athletes."

Tom Brady's tools as a left-handed-hitting catcher made scouts daydream. Then-Montreal Expos general manager Kevin Malone once said Brady's ability and makeup could have made him "one of the greatest catchers ever."

But scouts were so skeptical that he would sign, he was available for the Expos in the 18th round of the 1995 MLB draft. The scouts turned out to be right; Brady buried his catcher's mitt to chase glory in the Big House.

Wilson took baseball as far as Class A ball after the Colorado Rockies selected him 140th overall in 2010.

Rodgers played Little League baseball and made a local newspaper's front page as a free-throw shooting whiz at age 9.

Mahomes shagged fly balls in the outfield of major-league ballparks when he was barely taller than a bat, thanks to his father, Pat Sr., and his dad's best friend, LaTroy Hawkins. Both pitchers had lengthy big-league careers. Young Patrick played every imaginable sport with a ball, including golf and table tennis. He once knocked down a first baseman with a laser throw from shortstop.

Mahomes' counterpart in perhaps the greatest NFL game ever played — Kansas City's 42-36 playoff victory over Buffalo in January 2022 — also devoted his early years to multiple sports. When Josh Allen wasn't tending to chores on the family farm near Fresno, Calif., he participated in baseball, basketball, football, golf, gymnastics, karate and swimming, according to a 2017 ESPN.com story by Mark Schlabach. Allen led his high school basketball team in scoring and reached 90 mph on the mound.

Quinn also racked up K's with his right arm. He pitched and played outfield through his junior year at Dublin Coffman High School, outside Columbus, Ohio. He topped out in the high 80s before putting all his chips on football.

"There's nothing like playing quarterback," he says. "It is the greatest singular position in sports."

But playing a second sport such as baseball or basketball, Quinn insists, helps quarterbacks avoid burnout — and avoid the rush. When plays break down, athleticism and coordination matter even more.

Quinn has a spiritual brother in Joel Klatt, also a record-shattering college quarterback at Colorado with one of the nation's most prominent on-air college football gigs at Fox Sports.

Klatt's oldest son, Henry, is 10. Some of Henry's friends are already specializing, playing only football.

"Breaks my heart to see that," Klatt says. "When that happens, two things get lost: One, the ability to compete. I liked baseball and basketball (growing up), but what I really loved was competing. I wanted a scoreboard up, a winner and a loser. Two, there's a real risk of burnout."

Three, Klatt says, the skills learned on the basketball court, baseball diamond or lacrosse field are essential for future success. I mentioned Mahomes, Brady and Rodgers to Klatt. He added Justin Herbert, Matthew Stafford and Matt Ryan.

Herbert started on the basketball team as a sophomore at Sheldon High School in Oregon and pitched for its Class 6A state championship baseball team. He hit .400 and posted a 1.98 ERA in 42-plus innings.

Stafford was besties with future three-time Cy Young Award winner Clayton Kershaw in Dallas. They played on the same youth soccer, baseball, basketball and football teams. And when it was cold out, they played "hallway hockey" at Kershaw's house, as documented in a 2014 Bleacher Report story, with sawed-off hockey sticks, lines of tape to mark the goals and pillows for protection. They sometimes formed a battery in Little League baseball, with Kershaw firing the fastballs.

Ryan captained three sports at William Penn Charter School in Philadelphia: football, baseball and basketball. He played forward on the hardwood and multiple positions on the diamond, including shortstop and second base.

Upon graduating, this was Matt's message in his yearbook to his father, Mike: "Pop: thank you for your support and advice. I'll always remember to play with a bat, ball and a glove: not my mouth."

Klatt would not be surprised to hear that Ryan formed one-half of a double-play combo. After all, pitchers don't have to throw on the run.

"Great quarterback play is generally not (from) pitchers," Klatt says. "Playing quarterback is closer to being a middle infielder. You have to have the ability to change your arm angle, to dip, to move, to bend. That's way more valuable than trying to develop a repeatable delivery, as pitchers do.

"Think about Aaron Rodgers. At Cal he was rigid. Elbows up. Now his quarterback play is all about fluidity."

Quinn adds this on Rodgers: "His throwing motion, I don't know that you would teach it. If you slow it down, you can see he literally jumps when he throws. It's unique; it's how *he* does it. He creates vertical force with an unusual takeoff. It comes from being a dual-sport athlete. When kids give that stuff up, they stop learning how to (thrive) when things break down."

Quinn serves as an analyst on Fox Sports' college football pregame show, "Big Noon Kickoff," and provides color on college and NFL games for Fox. He could probably also jump into a baseball or basketball booth if needed.

"I played baseball, basketball and football growing up," he says. "My dad taught me how to throw — and throw *anything*. If I could pick it up, he taught me to throw it, from football to skipping rocks. I could throw hard at a young age."

Quinn grew up rooting for both the Reds and Indians in central Ohio. Young Brady was always going to games. And at home, father Ty took a block of firewood and turned it into a pitching rubber to create a 60-foot pathway. Ty insisted that Brady work from the stretch so he could develop arm strength and maintain accuracy with a tired arm.

"I threw every single day," he says.

Father and son analyzed pictures of Nolan Ryan in Sports Illustrated, noting the foot position and arm angles of a man who threw seven no-hitters and struck out 5,714 batters. Ty worked as a home builder, logging long hours and hustling to Brady's games.

"I'm in cleats holding a baseball bag (waiting to be picked up) and he'd say, 'Hey, I'm just around the corner.' I learned to warm up quick," Brady says with a chuckle. "We'd arrive at the field and he'd say, 'Hey, go down to the bullpen and make five or six throws.'"

Ty was such a strong athlete in high school, Brady says he could have played football or baseball in college. Instead he joined the Marines and served in Vietnam. At home, he was no drill sergeant.

"Dad always tried to make it fun," Brady says. "Everything was a competition. Most people play H.O.R.S.E. We applied that to football — we used a tree branch as a target or had to drop one in a trash can. He taught me that playing quarterback is about passing, not throwing."

At games, Dad was the calm one. As for Robin, Brady's mother ...

"My mom would find her way down to the sidelines, and if things were not going well she'd make sure to get in my line of sight to say how disappointed she was," Brady says. "In high school I'm thinking: How the hell did this lady get on the field? What cop or security guy let her down to the track? If I threw a pick, I'd grab water and hear her: 'Let's go! Get it together!'"

Both parents were vocal when it came to choosing a college. Brady grew up in Buckeye territory, but NFL quarterbacks didn't exactly sprout from Ohio State coach Jim Tressel's conservative game plans. The family visited Michigan, where legendary figure Bo Schembechler sized up Brady and asked: "Are you ready to go into Columbus and kick their ass?"

"My dad thought that was the coolest thing," Quinn recalls.

He sought an elite degree and chose Notre Dame, a four-hour drive from home, where he developed into the 22nd pick in the 2007 NFL draft. He and his father now blend their talents for the 3rd & Goal Foundation, which remodels living spaces for wounded veterans in need of enhancements such as wheelchair ramps.

Klatt also has a special relationship with his father, Gary, a revered figure at Pomona High School, outside Denver.

"My dad was a high school football coach for 30 years, and I always dreamed of playing for his team," Klatt says.

Joel learned football by hanging around practice and serving as a ballboy for games. But Gary did not let him play — even flag football — until eighth grade. By then Joel was a solid basketball player and emerging baseball prospect. He liked baseball. But he loved football "with all my heart," he says, perhaps because he had to wait so long to suit up.

"I'm a firm believer in the Gladwellian rule of achieving something great," he says. "I don't think people understand how much you have to pour into these tasks to even be a D1 football player. And if love is not fostered first, you will never commit to those 10,000 hours. I cringe when I see 9-year-olds starting to specialize. I think: Man, when you're 14, you're gonna hate it!"

At first, Joel envisioned himself playing linebacker, thirsting to hit ball carriers. But once it became clear he could throw, his father sacrificed. But not the way modern Quarterback Dads do. There were no trips to Vegas or Orlando for camps or clinics; these were simpler times.

"We didn't have much money, but he scraped together enough to buy five Wilson footballs," Klatt says. "He bought himself a pair of rodeo gloves so he wouldn't rip up his hands. He stood out there, and I threw thousands of footballs to him.

"We did very little technically. You know what he would do? He'd put his hands over his right shoulder ... then left shoulder ... then he'd go deep and ask for a touch ball. We never talked about *how* I was doing it, but I loved it. It was time with my dad."

Klatt played quarterback as a sophomore on the JV team, but as a junior he started only at safety. Today's Quarterback Dad might threaten a lawsuit if his son isn't running with the ones as a sophomore. Not Coach Klatt. "My dad said: 'You're not going to start over a senior (quarterback). That would be dumb.'"

That strategy hindered Klatt's college recruitment, as did his father's option-heavy offense. Joel dreamed of playing for Colorado State, but the Rams were not interested. Klatt didn't receive his first recruiting letter until November of his senior year and took visits to Northern Colorado, North Dakota State and South Dakota State.

"Playing earlier might have helped," he says. "And God love him, but my dad's offense was pretty archaic. But I wouldn't change it in hindsight."

Due in part to the cold shoulder from FBS schools, Klatt signed with the San Diego Padres after being drafted in the 11th round. He played first and third base but hit .209 and shut it down after two minor-league seasons. At 20, he walked on to Colorado's football team. He started for three seasons, set 19 school records, threw for 7,708 yards and earned All-Big 12 honors.

Now he breaks down quarterback play on Fox Sports and on Twitter @joelklatt.

He has three boys ranging in age from 5 to 10. They all play flag football, but Klatt is definitive upon being asked: Are you a Quarterback Dad?

"No," he says. "My sons get to play whatever sport they want. If they want me to help coach their team, they can ask. We're all about being active and having fun. My middle son plays baseball. My youngest wants to do hockey and lacrosse. They all swim. I'm always asked: Would you let your kids play football? The answer is they can play whatever they love."

Klatt is eternally grateful to his father, now retired in Colorado at age 76. Gary Klatt is a military man, like Ty Quinn. He served as a 2nd lieutenant in the Marines and did a 12-month tour in Vietnam, starting in 1969.

On the field, Klatt called his father "Coach." At home, "Dad." Never "sir."

"He said, 'I am your father, and this is not the military,'" Klatt says.

He carried a big stick. But he didn't use it.

Klatt grew up in a household where loving football was optional. Joel is now one of the premier voices in college football, calling Fox

Sports' No. 1 game. And older brother Jason is the head football coach at Colorado's Mead High School.

"My dad allowed me to fall in love with football — without his influence," Klatt says. "As a coach he was very hands off. He didn't handle the offense; he coached the defense. He cared way more about my character than the way I played."

CHAPTER 16

THE TACTICIAN QUARTERBACK DAD

Confession time: Greg Vandagriff could produce a better version of "Quarterback Dads" than the one you're reading.

I've been immersed in the topic for about two years. Vandagriff has lived it. He knows the difference between a "committable" and "noncommittable" offer. He knows why Nick Saban gets (almost) every recruit he covets and why some Power Five schools fail in the basics of the campus visit. He has ridden the emotional carousel stemming from son Brock's decision to switch his pledge from Oklahoma to Georgia. Some keyboard warriors on social media were not kind.

"The army of folks who come out of the woodwork to hate is unbelievable," he says. "You want to respond like Liam Neeson in 'Taken': I have a particular set of skills ..."

He's a high school coach who specializes in defense but sired and developed a five-star quarterback. He has an opinion on whether your son should play multiple sports and a take on whether you should steer him on his college selection.

He knows the dangers and delicacies of coaching his own flesh and blood, of handling bruised egos and crossing blurred lines. He speaks of a moment that left him speechless, when his dejected son eyed him after a baseball game and asked: "Can you just be my dad?"

He's striving to be a five-star Quarterback Dad after being around so many clueless ones.

"Most of them are obnoxious, unrealistic and can be really tough to be around," he says. "They think *they* are the guy who has the helmet on."

Chapter 3 of this book laid out 15 types of Quarterback Dads, from the "Demonstrator" to the "Hands-Off Dad."

Vandagriff belongs in a different category: He is the Tactician Dad. And not just as a Quarterback Dad. Oldest daughter Anna Greer earned a full ride to play volleyball at Eastern Kentucky. When younger sister Audrey hit a walk-off grand slam, her dad tweeted the clip and tagged the softball programs at Georgia, LSU, Tennessee and Alabama. She's the top-ranked non-pitcher in the 2024 class.

Brock's Twitter feed (@BrockVandagriff) reflects his father's advice on social media, which could be summarized in three words: Keep it vanilla.

"I tell 'em they can't 'like' anything controversial or political," Greg says. "Anything you put out is out there forever. You can't afford to make any strong statement — left or right. You can have opinions, but you better keep them to yourself. You don't know if (one day) you will be the No. 1-ranked player or the No. 5,000th-ranked player and no one will care what you think."

Brock takes an unusual approach to Twitter, especially for someone his age: Less is more. He tweets just a few times a month to his 13,000-plus followers. And instead of quoting rap lyrics, he'll quote a song he heard in church. Or retweet an accomplishment with the message "God is great."

Brock enrolled at Georgia in time for 2021 spring ball, and he participated in an intrasquad scrimmage on a Saturday in April. Greg turned down a friend's invitation to attend the third round of the Masters so he could watch the scrimmage in person.

Wait, he DID WHAT?

"If that's in the cards, it will happen another time," Greg says of roaming the grounds at Augusta National. "We get only one chance to be a parent. We've got to do this right."

The fact that Greg is the model Quarterback Dad is remarkable given that he didn't grow up with one.

"My dad spent 19 years in prison," he says. "I grew up in a trailer park and had every reason in the world to be a nobody. The way out for me was athletics. My mom and dad were not the presidents of the Touchdown Club. I played so I could put on a helmet and whip the guy's ass across from me. I could be better than him in football, maybe nothing else. Football was my release, my escape. I could not control what was going on at home, but I could control 3-6 p.m. on the field."

Greg's high school coach, Larry Kerr, inspired him not just to play football but eventually to become a high school coach: "If I could help a kid the way he helped me, it's a life worth living."

He has completed six seasons as head coach at Prince Avenue Christian School outside Athens, Ga. He has compiled a 69-11 record with one state title in the Class A Private division, a second appearance in the championship game in 2021 and three more trips to the semis.

He grew up in Knoxville, Tenn., and played free safety at Tennessee Wesleyan University. The unglamorous world of Division III ball, he says, is where the players love football "but it doesn't necessarily love them back."

Wife Kelly is an Auburn alumna who played junior college basketball. They agreed to a parenting philosophy counter to those in some youth sports organizations — no participation trophies.

Whether it was Chutes and Ladders, Sorry, Trouble or outdoor games such as Wiffle Ball or kickball, there would be no tanking to make the kids feel better.

Winning has consequences, and so does losing, Greg told them. You will circle the day you beat me. You will earn it.

And when the kids reached 12 or 13 years old, he suggested they follow one of two paths. He believes that age is perfect because that's when "small ball becomes big ball," when 200 feet down the left- and right-field lines becomes 280 feet. When bodies mature and kids have the inkling to make choices: Play for fun or play for a college scholarship.

I'm not going to chase it for you, Greg told his kids. You will chase it.

Brock grew up as a pitcher and quarterback. Father and son threw in the front yard so often, neighbors took note. Greg called Brock his "science experiment" but not in the Marv/Todd Marinovich kind of way: "You're telling me not having him drink a Diet Coke makes that much of a difference? Are you serious?!"

"I just wanted him to enjoy playing so he'd want to do it again next year," Greg says. "I told him: 'At some point if you're good enough, other people will notice.'"

Brock was the tallest kid on his flag football team, so he gravitated to quarterback. He played "pound" football from fourth to sixth grade, in which player weight helps determine rosters and positions. Greg noted that when linebackers rushed his son, Brock didn't lose his cool. He kept his eyes down the field, a sign he could cut it at the most difficult position in all of sports.

Brock also caught a break in middle school. His coach was Brad Johnson, who started 125 NFL games at quarterback over 15 seasons. And his top target became Brad's son Jake, now the top-ranked tight end in the Class of 2022 and a Texas A&M signee.

Before Brock entered high school, some friends suggested that Greg take him to the Duke football showcase run by coach David Cutcliffe, who mentored Peyton Manning at Tennessee. They explained that Greg had to "understand the dynamics," that he would be both entertained and floored. Not by the kids. By the dads.

There was the dad who held his kid back — for two academic years — resulting in a 6-foot-4 eighth-grader. Another dad was so aggressive in hiring and firing private trainers that within a few years, his son looked like Steve Sax trying to throw to first base. (Google it, kids.)

"Some of the dads strutted around like they were the players," Greg says. "Like they ought to charge admission just to hear them talk. It was unbelievable!

"And not only were there Quarterback Dads who were crazy and unrealistic and ruined kids' lives, there were trainers equally slimy, crazy and unrealistic."

It quickly became apparent that the behavior of the football dad mirrored the position of the son. You won't find many right tackle dads blasting the offensive coordinator on his son's team.

"Most of those kids are big and always have been big, so nobody messes with them," Greg says. "They play a position where they're in a supporting role, knights on the chess table, there to protect the king. Their role is to help, and they embrace that."

Greg subscribes to the "it takes a village" theory, saying he never feels like "the special sperm donor that created the perfect quarterback."

He served as the defensive coordinator for Brock's youth teams so he could be involved without having to call the plays. He did not want the head coach to unleash the "Brock Vandagriff show," as he put it, with Brock running it 30 times a game. He hoped that Brock would serve as a point guard, distributing the ball to the team's playmakers.

Meanwhile, he coordinated the defense and made what he believed was an ingenious arrangement with another dad/coach, given that kids resist advice from their own parents: "You correct my kid and I correct yours."

At one point Brock sniffed it out, ending the ruse.

The Duke camp also served to reinforce Greg's belief that Brock had talent. Greg was concerned he might be wearing "daddy goggles," which Urban Dictionary defines as "the tendency for dads to think their sons are way better athletes than they really are."

Greg asked Sam Pittman, then the offensive line coach at Georgia and now the head coach at Arkansas, for a brief evaluation.

Greg: Coach, you think he's any good?

Pittman: Tell you this, I'm writing his name down.

Brock showed equal promise on the diamond as a pitcher/third baseman/catcher. He hit well and threw better.

"Baseball and football are a good marriage," Greg says. "The seasons don't overlap, and you get two paths to chase a scholarship. If you put all the eggs in one basket, that's not a very good mentality until after your sophomore year."

Greg believed that if Brock had no football offers by the end of his sophomore year, he should focus on baseball. The problem with baseball, though, is that Division I teams typically divide 11.7 scholarships among 27 players.

"The money goes to pitching, and you only have so many bullets in that arm," Greg says. "Is it worth it to use 1,000 bullets (in a spring season), not counting warmups? We had a very real conversation: 'This is the risk and what you need to weigh.' We didn't treat him like an adult, but we also didn't sugarcoat it. I laid out the information like he was going to court."

Brock focused on football and debuted in August 2018 as a four-star recruit on 247Sports.com. The influential site's director of recruiting, Steve Wiltfong, says Greg believed Brock to be a five-star "but was never mean about it. Some dads get caught up in the rankings. He did not."

Within a year, Brock surged from the nation's 89th-ranked recruit to No. 7.

"I never got into it," Greg says of the rankings. "I didn't care. If you're always trying to fight someone's opinion, you will be miserable … like where my team is ranked at the start of a season. Who cares?"

With offers pouring in from every top Power Five program, it was time for Brock to form a list and for the family to visit schools. His dad told him: "Form your own opinion. And then when you're serious about it, ask me."

And this: "You will choose the school because one night you will be lying in bed after you throw three interceptions and they're screaming: 'Brock, you suck!' ... You will have to live with that choice. You can't blame your dad and say: 'I didn't want to come here. You made me go.'"

Brock briefly considered Michigan because of a connection to then-defensive coordinator Don Brown. But the family honed in on schools in the ACC (Clemson, Miami, North Carolina), SEC (Alabama, Georgia, Auburn, Tennessee, Mississippi State, Arkansas) and Oklahoma.

Auburn didn't stand a chance because the family believes Gus Malzahn, who was fired after the 2020 season and now coaches at UCF, is incapable of developing NFL quarterbacks. (Cam Newton, a wondrous talent, transferred in from Florida via Blinn College.)

Visits to Arkansas and Mississippi State revealed why those schools remain second- or third-class citizens in the SEC. The golf cart the Vandagriffs were given to tour around the Starkville campus was soaking wet from rain, and no one on the Razorbacks staff bothered to meet them when they arrived on campus. So they spent 30 minutes lost, looking for the football office.

The visit to Tuscaloosa stood in direct contrast. Every aspect reflected Saban's obsession with detail. Greg was instructed to call a graduate assistant once the family exited the highway. The GA guided them to campus, where he awaited their arrival. He directed them to a hostess in a golf cart, which occupied their parking spot.

"We're driven to the front door, where a coach meets us and hands me a card with our itinerary for the next five hours," Greg recalls. "Wow!"

First up: a meeting with Saban.

"The godfather," Greg jokes. "We didn't know how to act. Do we bow? Make eye contact? Turns out he was a down-to-earth guy, super normal.

"They bring us in there. After 15 minutes the door rattles, and the secretary is giving him an 'out.' Very polished. We know the deal and he ignores her. She comes back 15 minutes later, and he ignores her. Third time, he says to her: 'Thanks for letting me know, I'll be right there.'"

Brad Johnson, who played at Florida State before throwing 166 NFL touchdown passes and coaching Brock in middle school, warned the family they would leave Saban's office unsure of whether he actually had offered a scholarship. And that's exactly what happened.

"You never hear: We want you to know you have an offer," Greg says. "It's: Obviously we believe you can play here …"

The Vandagriffs enjoyed visiting Clemson, but the Tigers coaches slow-rolled them, saying they wouldn't make an offer until Brock's junior year. Meanwhile, Greg told Clemson quarterbacks coach Brandon Streeter that Brock would not come if D.J. Uiagalelei, the top-ranked pro-style quarterback in the 2020 class, committed. The family had just watched the Jake Fromm/Justin Fields drama play out at Georgia, with Fields transferring to Ohio State, and wanted no part of something similar.

"Your son doesn't want to compete?" Streeter asked.

"It's not that," Greg replied. "It's common sense. Do we want to ruin D.J.'s life? Or our son's life?"

The family made the 14-hour trip to Norman, Okla., and were blown away by every aspect of the Sooners program, including coach Lincoln Riley's emphasis on postgraduation plans. "It was like: Holy cow!" Greg says. "You can see why they are ultrasuccessful."

Brock verbally committed to Oklahoma in the summer of 2019, but the family had misgivings about the distance to campus. Every game, home and away, would be a road game, costing about $1,000 out of pocket. And how would they attend Anna Greer's volleyball matches or Audrey's softball games? They might be able to visit Brock just once or twice a season.

The family attended Oklahoma's 2019 game against West Virginia and were horrified to see the Sooner Schooner crash on the field. The horse-drawn wagon, filled with passengers, tipped over after a sharp turn.

They took that as a sign. Greg called it "foreshadowing ... the football gods trying to communicate."

Then they attended the Dec. 28, 2019, semifinal playoff game in Atlanta and watched as LSU's Joe Burrow fired seven first-half touchdown throws. As Greg put it, the Sooners "got drug up and down the field."

Over Christmas break, Brock expressed that he wanted to play for Georgia, saying: "Everything I want can be found in the SEC."

His father told him that was fine but that this decision would be final: "We don't want you getting a rep of 'He can't make a commitment.' You are creating your own brand right now, getting judged on every decision you make."

He decommitted from Oklahoma on Jan. 1, 2020. Three weeks later he pledged to Georgia with a simple announcement on Twitter: "I'm staying home. #GoDawgs #CommitToTheG."

Brock told Rusty Mansell of 247Sports: "To walk away from Lincoln Riley and Oklahoma was not an easy thing to do. We were sitting around the dinner table (at Thanksgiving) and my grandmother made the comment about how far Oklahoma was. It was funny she said that because it had been on my mind privately."

Vandagriff said he also got assurances from Bulldogs offensive coordinator Todd Monken that "he wants to bring more passing to Georgia ... what he is about to do with the Georgia offense is going to be awesome."

Georgia coaches had stayed in touch with Brock through Twitter and Instagram. That's typical. They knew they had a chance with the hometown kid.

Oklahoma also protected itself. Schools must do that in this era of commitments, decommitments, recommitments, etc.

Six months after Vandagriff's decommitment, the Sooners got a pledge from Caleb Williams, the nation's top-ranked pro-style quarterback. (Chapter 18 chronicles his story.) Vandagriff was ranked No. 3, Michigan's J.J. McCarthy No. 4.

"If you don't believe those back-channel conversations are happening, you are delusional," Greg says. "The hardest thing to understand as a Quarterback Dad is that what they are telling you, they are also telling the next kid who plays his position. They like your kid one day and someone else's the next."

Along the way, the Vandagriffs got an education in recruiting. They learned the difference between a "committable" and "noncommittable" offer. The latter comes with this caveat: "We really like you, but we want to see your junior film."

They also learned the cold reality of what some schools do. A quarterback verbally commits, and the coach replies: Great! Keep it quiet while we get to work on our social media. We want this to blow up.

The second the phone call ends, that coach calls a quarterback prospect ranked higher on his board and tells him: Hey, Joe Blow is ready to commit to us. You need to let us know by tomorrow.

"The toughest thing to know as a Quarterback Dad," Greg says, "is that only one can play at a time."

It's a stressful process. But let's be honest: Much of youth sports is, especially for those ultimately seeking a college scholarship.

Greg thinks about all the times a player has told him after a game or practice that he is dreading the car ride home. He knows his father will berate him.

And once upon a time, Greg was that dad. He recalls when Brock was 10 and played poorly in a Little League baseball game.

"We get in the car and I can't wait to correct him," he says. "He looks at me and says: 'Can you just be my dad?' It hit me like a ton of bricks.

"What's more important, me coaching him or me being his dad? Growing up without a dad, 19 years in prison, I said: 'You know what, Brock? From now on, if you want to talk about the ballgame, we will. But if you want to talk about getting a Slushee, we'll do that. Son, I love you. All I care about is being your dad.'"

CHAPTER 17

'WHEN YOU MEET YOU'

"OK, come here," Donovan Dooley tells a dozen high school quarterbacks and receivers after a workout. "Let's talk for a quick second."

That quick second turns into a powerful 17-minute lecture that features this piercing question: "What are you gonna do when you meet you?"

The players form a semicircle around Dooley and Levi Bradley, a skilled connector in the mold of basketball's William Wesley, aka World Wide Wes.

They've been slinging and catching balls in suburban Chicago on a sun-splashed fall day. With the COVID-19 pandemic having harpooned their 2020 football seasons, pop-up sessions like this offer a chance to stay sharp and provide film for social media.

"Look, I thought that was good work," Dooley tells them. "It's important to get any nuggets of wisdom you can. I know a lot of times I repeat myself, but you have to take that. If you make a mistake with a coach, try to make a new mistake. Don't make the same damn mistake."

Dooley says the players who continue to make the same mental mistakes will be labeled uncoachable. And if you're a mid-level high school prospect deemed uncoachable, you might as well join the band.

The group contains several impressive prospects, including two three-star recruits from Kenwood Academy: Lewis Bond and Jalil Martin.

117

"A lot of you guys are headed to play big-time football," Dooley says. "I ask you: What are you going to do when you meet you? When a guy has the same size, speed and intellect as you but has put more film study in? He has put more into the craft and is gaming you."

When you meet you.

If these prospects don't immediately understand the concept, they will.

Dooley cannot fathom the thought of any of his pupils being less prepared than their competition.

"I've seen some good shit from you guys," he says. "But one thing I'd encourage you to do is ask more questions. You guys don't ask enough questions. Anytime I go somewhere and I think there's a valuable resource, I ask a million questions. 'Cause that's gonna make me an animal!

"There might be two or three people who came up with something. The RPOs (run-pass options) were innovative. But football is all stealin'. If I go to your guys' school and see a unique system or scheme, I'm gonna steal it! So be crafty."

He pauses and asks: "Anybody got any questions on anything? I don't care what it is ... anything?"

Silence.

"Y'all know it all, huh? Y'all good? No questions, nothing?"

Silence.

"That's what I'm saying!"

Dooley has been inquisitive since he was 8 and a coach named Steve Collins told him: "Once you believe you know it all, that's the beginning of the end."

"I took that shit to heart," Dooley says. "When a coach gave a protection scheme, I wanted to know why."

He asks Bond: "What's the weak part of your game?"

Bond replies softly: "Probably going in and out of my break."

Dooley: "I didn't hear you!"

"OK, if I was to ask you coverages zero through six, what would you say? You see that dead silence right there? That's your weakness! You feel me? That's the thing a college coach will do to you? What if he asks you, 'What's your favorite play on third-and-7 versus a cover-2?'"

Bond replies: "Gimme the ball."

Dooley: "That ain't good enough!"

"Listen," he continues. "What are you gonna do when you meet you?! What if he's playing hard inside with a capped safety over the top?! So he's got field pressure and he's going to drive inside and he's got help from one? You ain't got shit coming, son! You may win the route, but he's gonna knock your head off when you reach for it! So you have to understand when someone asks for the weak part of your game … for a lot of you guys, it's coverage. You don't understand the field. You understand me versus you when it's man-free (man-to-man coverage plus a free safety)."

Dooley is rolling.

"But what are you gonna do when the defensive end starts dropping into coverage? When they're sending corner-cat? OK, who knows what corner-cat means? (A cornerback blitz.) A lot of teams run corner-cat when the ball's on a certain hash. You have to understand space.

"I know you guys go to a million camps and y'all like to do one-on-ones. OK, lemme run this corner post or this 'circus' (made-up) route. Quarterbacks don't have much time. We've got 1.8 to 2.4 (seconds) to get rid of this football. With a muddy pocket. Don't forget this is a team sport."

He turns to Bond.

"The thing I loved about you today is when I said, 'Run a route,' you asked, 'What's the coverage?' When I met you, you weren't asking that."

He then introduces Bradley, a recruiting adviser whom he refers to as "Coach Levi."

Bradley tells them about Miles Scott, a Chicago-area prospect who declined an offer from Army to become a preferred walk-on at Illinois.

"They say he is a problem, a nightmare," Bradley says, using "problem" and "nightmare" in the most complimentary sense. "When he gets done dishragging everybody at practice, he gets on YouTube and studies.

"The kid with the most knowledge is the guy who's gonna play."

Bradley, a matchmaker who prides himself on helping both recruits and college coaches, tells the story of Michael Floyd, who holds Notre Dame records for career (271) and single-season (100) receptions and was drafted in the first round by the Cardinals. Floyd grew up in Minneapolis, where Bradley has a strong presence.

"I had Mike Floyd and the thing is, he's super-duper intelligent," Bradley says. "Yeah, he's 6-foot-3½ and can jump out the gym and can catch. When he went to Notre Dame, he said: 'I'm gonna break every record.' You know how he got 'em? It wasn't just being tall and long. He studied the game like you wouldn't believe. He said: 'Dawg, I come from the struggle, I need to get this money and I've got three years to do it!'

"Y'all hear me talk about Larry Fitzgerald all the time. We grew up together (in Minneapolis). I was talking to him last week. The thing I liked about Larry — he's a dude who knew he was slow and is still slow to this day. But he can run routes and he can catch and he's tough as nails. He's like: I ain't no punk. I can catch. And I know football.

"Intelligence? Larry wasn't that dude in the classroom, but when it came to football, he made sure he knew everything. He could see guys line up and be just as intelligent as a quarterback. ... He figured out: The more I know, the better off I'm gonna be because I'm not fast. That's all he'd say: I'm not fast. But he attracts that ball, he adjusts, his hand-eye coordination is stupid. It's a gift.

"So be more knowledgeable. Asking questions makes a huge difference. This COVID situation has changed the game and messed it up for everyone, but I'm proud of you guys for finding a way to get work. Take advantage of the work you can get."

And don't forget ...

"Ask questions," Dooley says. "The more you know on the field, the faster you will be able to play. I promise you."

Bond selected Boston College and enrolled early in January 2021. He appeared in two games as a freshman, making a 6-yard catch against NC State.

Martin committed to Boston College and ended up with a dozen Power Five offers. He signed with Nebraska, where he hopes to get playing time in the fall.

CHAPTER 18

THE QUARTERBACK DAD WITH ANSWERS

The turning point of Caleb Williams' football career came at the tender age of 11. It's the moment his dad transformed into a Quarterback Dad.

Williams was playing running back for an all-star team representing Maryland, gashing defenses for nearly 15 yards a carry. He didn't ask to play quarterback because he was uninterested in the position's responsibilities.

One day he had to miss practice. And that happened to be the day his coach installed a new pass-happy, one-back offense. Williams would not be that starting back. The coach apparently felt he was too small.

The team lost, and the quarterback — the coach's son (what a coincidence!) — screamed and moaned as he exited the field. Caleb was upset too. He was so angry, he broke down and refused to ride on the team bus back to the hotel. He was distraught over not being able to affect the game.

Carl Williams, Caleb's father, was stunned. The tears were a jarring sight.

"From the time the doctor smacked him," Carl jokes, "he had probably cried twice. His mom (Dayna) and I didn't know what to do."

She flew back to D.C. on the flight's lone open seat. Caleb and Carl stayed up in their San Antonio hotel room, talking and strategizing. Their session lasted till 2 a.m. By the end of it, a star was born.

Caleb announced he wanted to be a quarterback. Not only that, he declared: "I want to be the best to ever play the game."

Carl replied: "If you just want to run around, that's one thing. If you want to be the best, there is only one way. Your life has to change. You have to train daily. Change your diet; no fast food. Work on your skills — speed, power and agility. You have to know what the defense is doing and why. And you're not a little white kid, so you're going to have to get beyond the stereotypes. But most importantly, outwork everybody."

Caleb soaked it in and they agreed to take the journey together.

Carl mainly works as a real estate developer, but he and two of Caleb's mentors decided to expand the portfolio by opening a training center in Maryland. The programs at Athletic Republic emphasize speed, power, agility and "increasing the competitive skills required to become a champion."

Says Carl: "When a kid decides he has a dream and is willing to work for it, you turn over whatever resources you have. As a parent you make the investment, you adjust your life. Honestly, it doesn't matter if you have to refinance or take out a second mortgage. If you want uncommon results, you have to do uncommon things."

Carl's own dreams of becoming an NFL or NBA player ended when he blew out his knee in high school. In the early '80s, that could be the death knell for a young athlete.

"I figured I would get bigger and stronger and walk on (at college) and get back to my wannabe superstar self," he says, "but it didn't work out that way."

Instead, his education-minded parents (he says his mother graduated from high school at age 15) enrolled him at Emerson Prep, a tiny private school in Washington, D.C., that did not offer sports. His father was a pastor, active in the civil rights movement.

Even before Carl wrecked his knee, his father rarely saw him compete in youth sports. He was busy fighting for a larger cause.

"My dad did not have time on Saturdays to come to many of my ballgames," Carl says, "so I made it a point to never miss a game of Caleb's. Ever."

OK, one time he missed a half. Carl had to make a presentation, and the meeting ran long. He had an assistant bring his car around. He tried to push the participants, asking: "Are those all the questions? Are we all set?"

Then he sped off.

"I did 120 on the Beltway," he says.

All so he wouldn't miss too much of Caleb's middle-school game.

Passive is not a word you'd use to describe Carl's style of parenting. After Caleb made his declaration at age 11, Carl devoted his energy to giving his son every conceivable advantage: "Hell or high water, we'd throw 100 balls a day. It was his dream to be the best possible athlete — and best possible quarterback. So we'd find the best possible trainer."

Four times a week, including Saturday, Carl had Caleb wake up at 4:30 a.m. for what they called "The Breakfast Club." From 5:30-7, Caleb worked out with high school athletes, building his physique and improving his speed.

"He liked it," Carl said. "He was competitive."

He bought in. Carl remembers a night when Caleb was in seventh grade. He was texting with a girl who asked him to call her. Caleb replied: *Sorry, I've got to train tomorrow.*

"Brought a little tear to my eye," Carl says. "I thought: The kid gets it."

And the dad made sure to stay in his lane. He never coached any of Caleb's youth teams, concerned he would get too wound up on the sidelines.

"I could never do that because I would be the Bobby Knight of football," he says with a chuckle. "I'd rather be helpful, supportive and buy the whole team Gatorade after."

Which is not to say that Carl is relaxed when Caleb is on the field: "I'm a nervous wreck and try to stay away from people as much as possible. As a Quarterback Dad, you are in control or at least feel like you are. The game starts and you lose complete control of everything."

Carl began enlisting private quarterback trainers when Caleb was 10. He worked with Chris Baucia of QB Factory and several gurus at QB Collective, including Will Hewlett. A 2018 Washington Post story detailed Williams' year-round pursuit of excellence.

"No summers off," Caleb said. "This is what I do."

Carl and Caleb traveled to camps all over America, including one hosted by Russell Wilson at USC. Recruiters and coaches became so familiar with Caleb, he was on schools' recruiting boards in the eighth grade. Maryland offered him a scholarship before he entered high school.

The Williams family paid about $25,000 a year so Caleb could attend Gonzaga College High School, the prestigious all-boys Catholic school within a mile of the Capitol Building. It was there that the quarterback's legend grew. And his nickname took hold: "Superman."

There was the game during which he threw for a touchdown, ran for a touchdown and caught a touchdown pass. One time in practice, he cracked the wedding ring of a coach who had the gall to try to catch one of his ropes.

But Caleb really earned his cape on the final night of his sophomore season, when three touchdowns were scored in the final 29 seconds of a league championship game against Maryland powerhouse DeMatha. Williams launched a 60-plus-yard Hail Mary that found the arms of teammate John Marshall. Winner!

Caleb embraces the nickname. The dominant image on his Twitter page is the spelled-out version of the Superman logo, gold lettering across a black background.

It's funny. Caleb's mother, Dayna Price, wanted "Superman" to be his middle name. Carl countered that he might have to get a job one day, and that would look weird on an application. So they settled on

Sequan for the sake of the "S" — even though Carl says he doesn't know how Dayna came up with it.

Caleb was so active as an infant, he would climb to the top of his crib and jump off. "Like Superman," Carl says.

A massive Sports Illustrated piece in October 2021 described Williams as "the new face of a changing game" — a fashionista who paints his nails, wrote a blog for SI.com during high school and makes brilliant use of social media. More than 110,000 follow his Instagram account, and his pinned tweet reads: "I'm Not a Businessman; I'm a Business, Man!"

In August 2021 the family applied for four trademarks: Caleb Williams' name, a logo featuring his CW initials, a silhouette after Williams releases a pass and a Superman-like logo featuring the CW initials. They cannot, of course, use the actual Superman symbol.

"We don't have a deal with Warner Brothers, at least not yet," Carl jokes.

The Williams family took a methodical, businesslike approach to Caleb's recruitment and ultimate selection of Oklahoma. As detailed in a Yahoo Sports piece by Pete Thamel, Carl created a spreadsheet broken into four categories: ACADEMICS, ATHLETICS, PREPARATION and INTANGIBLES.

Subcategories included value of degree (academics), commitment to quarterback development (athletics), strength and conditioning/hot yoga (preparation) and connection to the coaching staff (intangibles).

Carl asked every school to detail how it could propel his son to become the No. 1 pick in the 2024 NFL draft. He has a beef with programs that do not, in his view, balance the goals of winning and player development. He cited Mississippi State coach Mike Leach and his "glorified high school offense" that consistently produces winning seasons but also a trail of NFL ghosts (B.J. Symons, Cody Hodges, Graham Harrell, Luke Falk).

"If you go to medical school, you should be prepared to be a doctor," Carl says. "If you go to law school, you should be prepared to be a lawyer."

The Williams family was patient during the recruiting process. When five-star recruit Brock Vandagriff (Chapter 16) switched his commitment from Oklahoma to Georgia, a slot opened in Norman. Then again, the Williams family does not fear competition.

They were unmoved that Oklahoma's incumbent quarterback, Spencer Rattler, entered the 2021 season as the Heisman Trophy favorite. On top of that, Carl asserted that he was willing to have his son walk on if he were convinced the fit was right but no scholarships remained.

Sooners coach Lincoln Riley had the credentials after pupils Baker Mayfield and Kyler Murray were both taken No. 1 in their respective drafts and rookie Jalen Hurts supplanted Carson Wentz as the Philadelphia Eagles starter in 2020. As a bonus, Riley had a scholarship available.

Williams officially selected Oklahoma on July 4, 2020, in a manner befitting a five-star quarterback who enjoys the spotlight. CBS Sports produced a cinematic, two-minute piece for social media that featured Williams in front of various D.C. landmarks. It closed with images of fireworks and the first-person narrator saying: "In the end, it's the hardest choices that matter the most. One more choice ..."

Williams then emerged, wearing a Sooners jersey. The banner read: CALEB WILLIAMS COMMITS TO OKLAHOMA.

That summer, Caleb and Carl created what they called the Sooner Summit. He invited Oklahoma commits and recruits to Norman so they could tour the campus and get to know one other in the face of COVID-19 restrictions. His inspiration was the film "One Night in Miami," a fictionalized account of a 1964 meeting of Malcolm X, Muhammad Ali, Jim Brown and musical performer Sam Cooke.

"We did our own campus tour," Carl recalls. "We couldn't get into the football (training) facility, but we did get into the stadium. And we created a bond."

Upon returning home, the Williams family faced a tough decision.

With D.C. experiencing some of the nation's most stringent COVID protocols, Gonzaga canceled the 2020 football season. Schools all over the nation reached out, but Carl and Caleb took a different route.

With Gonzaga limited to remote learning, Carl moved his son to Norman. In January 2021, Caleb dual-enrolled at Gonzaga and Oklahoma, creating a load of 11 classes. On top of that, Caleb participated in spring practice.

"He was the first guy in the building," Carl says, "and the last one to leave."

Williams outplayed Rattler in the spring game. So whenever Rattler struggled in the fall of 2021, parts of the student section would chant: "We want Caleb!"

The wish was granted in OU's sixth game, with the Sooners trailing archrival Texas 28-7. Williams led his team on nine scoring drives in a 55-48 victory that had America googling "Superman" for a new reason. Williams finished with 212 passing yards, 88 rushing yards and an ESPN QB Rating of 97.5 on a 100-point scale. Rattler's QBR was 8.9.

Williams finished the season as the nation's fifth-ranked quarterback in passing efficiency, two spots ahead of Heisman Trophy winner Bryce Young. But Riley's stunning decision to leave for USC made him re-evaluate.

For weeks, the Twitterati speculated on his next move. Former NFL quarterback Charlie Batch tweeted that his company, GameAbove Capital, would pay Williams $1 million to play for Batch's alma mater, Eastern Michigan. Deadspin guessed Williams was going to North Carolina in a story under the headline, "Let's use the Girlfriend Transfer Portal Theory to figure out where Caleb Williams is headed."

USC emerged as the favorite even though the Williams family was disappointed that Riley did not contact them when he announced the move. When Caleb was notified of an emergency meeting on Nov. 28, he figured it was regarding the Sooners' appearance in the Alamo Bowl.

Williams buried Oregon in the Alamo Bowl (21-for-27, 242 yards, 3 TDs, 0 INTs) and then dug in on his decision: Should I stay or should I go?

Many figured it would come down to finances — i.e., where Caleb could most effectively cash in on his NIL (name, image and likeness). Carl quickly debunked that.

"It's NFL, not NIL," he says. "The first pick in the draft last year came close to $40 million ($36.8 million for Trevor Lawrence). And the fact of the matter is, in 2024, there will be a significant bump in the salary cap."

Williams formed that conclusion by analyzing projected revenue surges from sports betting companies and expiring media rights agreements. The deals for Fox, CBS and NBC lapse in 2023.

"That's what I do as a Quarterback Dad," Carl says. "You do the research, you find the answers."

And, sometimes, form multiple-choice questions. Coaches from more than 25 schools inquired, and Carl gave every one an audience, primarily by Zoom. He mentioned each school to Caleb and then whittled the list.

Wisconsin impressed the Williamses by hiring Bobby Engram, who has an NFL pedigree and ties to the family, as its offensive coordinator. And the Badgers emphasized how NC State transfer Russell Wilson thrived in Madison under current head coach Paul Chryst.

UCLA also made a strong push, with Carl calling coach Chip Kelly "an offensive mastermind."

In the end, L.A. won. Just not UCLA.

Caleb chose USC, marking the second time Riley had won over the family. He apologized for leaving them in the dark while citing the NCAA's tampering rules. Head coaches are technically not permitted to contact players from other schools until they enter the transfer portal. Williams did not do that until Jan. 4.

On the day Caleb committed, USC went from 50-1 to 25-1 to win the national title, according to PointsBet sportsbook. And his Heisman Trophy odds dropped from 14-1 to 8-1, third behind Young and Ohio State's C.J. Stroud.

Winning — and winning a Heisman — were huge factors. But perhaps not as big as Caleb's development as both a quarterback and a young man. Carl encouraged his son to focus on overall growth.

"For us it goes beyond football," Carl says. "The average pro career is less than four years. What will you do when it's over? It's great if you can make a billion dollars playing ball, but what will you do when that is over? What else interests you? How do you become a more well-rounded person?"

Caleb's interests include fashion, television and business. He'll be near Hollywood. He can access Rodeo Drive. USC has a top-20 business school, and Carl mentioned its new Iovine and Young Academy — the Young is Andre "Dr. Dre" Young — that focuses on entrepreneurship and hands-on learning.

"You only get two more years," Carl says. "This is your last time to be a kid and to do what college kids do."

Carl loves that Caleb played in one of college football's biggest games, the Red River Rivalry, and now will play in one of its most storied venues, the Coliseum — with a Nov. 19, 2022, date at the Rose Bowl against UCLA. But ultimately, he says, this was not his dream. It was his son's.

Asked if they made the decision jointly, Carl pauses and replies: "The answer is, it was entirely Caleb's choice. His mentors and I narrowed things down. At the end of the day, this is his journey and he made the final decision."

CHAPTER 19

ADVICE FROM BIG TEN COACHES

At one time Pat Fitzgerald and Bret Bielema were the two youngest head coaches in the Big Ten. "Part of the Atari generation," Fitzgerald jokes.

They've seen some things. Heard some things. Formed bonds with terrific Quarterback Dads. Rolled their eyes at overbearing Quarterback Dads.

"The most frustrating thing in recruiting sometimes is not the 18-year-old kid," Bielema says, "but the 38-year-old dad."

"There are great ones, good ones and bad ones," Fitzgerald says. "The challenging ones are living vicariously through their son. They're being a helicopter parent and making it very challenging for the young person to learn and grow.

"The good ones are supportive; they understand this is their child's life and they do everything they can to help and support that. They are more parent than superfan."

Fitzgerald is entering his 17th season as Northwestern's head coach. He picked up National Coach of the Year honors after the Wildcats won the Big Ten West in 2020. Bielema came to Illinois with strong credentials, having guided Wisconsin to three straight Rose Bowls from 2010-12. After getting pink-slipped at Arkansas, he worked alongside Bill Belichick with the New England Patriots.

Illinois hired him in December 2020 to replace Lovie Smith, and Bielema rewarded the Illini with stunning road victories over Penn

State and Minnesota in 2021. The season ended with a 47-14 trouncing of Fitzgerald's Wildcats and the satisfaction of having helped to revitalize the career of quarterback Brandon Peters.

Peters, the sixth-year senior who ventured to Arizona for that predawn workout at Kurt Warner's compound (Chapter 1), has as level-headed a Quarterback Dad as any on the planet.

"We have a saying in our family: Keep clear eyes," David Peters says. "You've got people kissing your butt when things are going great and then those same people are talking smack if things go sideways. People love to see you succeed and also love to see you fail."

Peters did both during a three-year stint at Michigan, replacing John O'Korn during the 2017 season and beating Rutgers, Minnesota and Maryland with a low-risk style: four TD passes, zero interceptions. A week later he not only suffered a concussion at Wisconsin, he blacked out.

After Peters struggled in the bowl game against South Carolina (20-for-44, 2 INTs), things were never the same with the Michigan coaches. In the offseason they got a shiny new toy in Shea Patterson, a transfer from Ole Miss. Peters got relegated to third string in 2018, attempting two passes all season.

But Peters didn't gripe. Nor did his father, who puts it like this: "If you want fair, go downtown to the state fair."

After transferring to Illinois and experiencing some ups and downs under Smith in 2019 and 2020, Peters entered the 2021 season as the Illini's top quarterback. Then he got sacked in the opener by a 295-pound Nebraska tackle and separated his left shoulder. Six weeks later Wisconsin dinged him again, leaving him with torn cartilage in his ribs.

He didn't practice the week of the Penn State game, traveling to State College as an emergency backup. He got summoned in the seventh overtime — you read that right — and fired the game-winner in the ninth overtime of a 20-18 victory.

Finally healthy again and facing his football mortality, Peters could practically count the grains of sand left in the hourglass. Bielema sought him out to say: "You've got four games left, do or die, to get in the league. You have four games to express yourself."

Something clicked. Peters played efficiently against Rutgers and Minnesota, completing a combined 21 of 28 passes for 270 yards with three TDs and no picks. Iowa picked him off twice, but Peters shined against Northwestern, throwing for 242 yards. He talked enough smack and showed so much moxie that when his father looked down from his Memorial Stadium suite, he thought: That's not our son.

"He's a kid who has been smacked in the face," his father says, "but he keeps coming back."

After that win over Northwestern, Bielema told the Big Ten Network: "I can't say enough about his growth and how he led the huddle today. Since he came back in the lineup, his preparation, his detail, his fire, his energy … hopefully he has put himself in position to get a shot at that next level."

Bielema says that while recruiting quarterbacks, he tells every dad: "When we have great success, your son will get more credit. When we have failure, he will get more criticism. I will always praise and protect him (publicly) and never put the game on him."

Two of the best Quarterback Dads that Bielema encountered were Mike Tolzien and Harrison Wilson III. Scott Tolzien went 21-5 as a starter for Wisconsin, and Russell Wilson is, well, Russell Wilson. He had one of the greatest statistical seasons in college football history for the Badgers before becoming an eight-time Pro Bowler in Seattle.

Bielema recalled that Harrison Wilson III passed away the day after his son was drafted by the Colorado Rockies. Harrison was an attorney who played football and baseball at Dartmouth. He died at 55 after having suffered from diabetes.

Russell Wilson told ESPN.com for a 2020 story that his father encouraged him to dream big: "When I was young, he used to always ask me the question: 'Son, why not you? Why don't you play pro base-ball? Why don't you play pro football?' The idea of 'Why not you?' was really at the center of who I was. I started really subconsciously and consciously asking myself that question."

Bielema got choked up on the phone recalling a letter of gratitude he received from Mike Tolzien. His simple message: Thank you for what you did for my son.

Asked to share advice for Quarterback Dads, Bielema relayed the following:

1. "The more sports he can play, the better. If he learns to lead in all sports, he will be better at the one he specializes in. The quarterback should be the captain of the baseball team, the basketball team and the football team. Be in those leadership positions — point guard, shortstop or pitcher."

2. "Have him work on his communication skills, even acting skills. Scott Tolzien was a quiet kid, but his teammates would do anything for them. You could tell that in moments of adversity."

3. "Don't always put your son in a position of success. He doesn't have to play for the best 7-on-7 team. Try to make him stress. When Russell Wilson was with us, he sometimes faced a defensive concept he hadn't seen (in practice or on film) on third-and-6. Not only did we not know what he would do, the defense didn't know."

4. "Don't plan out every stage. Let him have his own path. Let him be normal; don't protect him. He's got to be able to fall off his bike and break his arm."

5. Don't be the dad who still obsesses over his own career and claims that his coaches prevented him from success. "Maybe you weren't good enough, my friend."

Here are Fitzgerald's top three pieces of advice for Quarterback Dads:

1. "Let him breathe. Let him be a kid. I tell our coaches all the time: We do this for a living and *we're* still not great at it."

2. "Get to know your kids and have a relationship with them. That way you'll know when it's time to push, when it's time to hug and when it's time to give 'em a kick in the britches."

3. "When you're looking into the face mask, never forget what it was like to look out of the face mask. Never forget what it's like to be a player, an eighth-grader or a high school kid. When you were them, would you have wanted your dad at practice? Would you have wanted him hovering over you? Maybe you feel your son needs that type of direction or guidance. But it's my experience that at some point that young little chick is gonna leave the nest. The young eagle will spread its wings to soar. Teach him those life skills."

Fitzgerald said he's never had a bad Quarterback Dad during his entire time at Northwestern. Luck of the draw? Hardly. His staffers weed out potential headaches before their sons reach an advanced stage of recruitment.

"It's a major part of our evaluation," he says. "I would tell you that we don't have to evaluate our offensive linemen's parents the same way we evaluate the quarterbacks' parents. The offensive linemen are typically 'team' guys who don't care if their names get called."

Fitzgerald calls quarterbacking "the most difficult position to play in major college or professional sports," and he's tuned in to how the player will respond to adversity: "Who is their support network? When it gets hard, who are they gonna call? When they call home, will the response (from Dad) be: Keep working hard, keep grinding, get in the film room, get with the older players?"

No? Then Fitzgerald might cross that player off his recruiting list.

"I'll ask the dads: Describe who you will be as a Quarterback Dad," he says. "Some of the answers are fascinating. From some you can tell: This rascal's gonna be a handful. Do I really want to have to deal with that?"

Fitzgerald mentions the great dads he has dealt with, including the fathers of Mike Kafka, Dan Persa, Matt Alviti, Trevor Siemian, Clayton Thorson, TJ Green and Peyton Ramsey. Doug Ramsey is the acclaimed high school coach in Cincinnati who believed Northwestern should have offered Peyton a scholarship out of high school (Chapter 9). The Wildcats QB coach preferred Aidan Smith, a better athlete.

Smith bombed in 2019, prompting Fitzgerald to seek help from the transfer portal. Ramsey was available after three seasons at Indiana.

"When we decided not to offer Peyton (out of high school), Doug said: 'I think you'll see that he will end up being a really good player,'" Fitzgerald recalls. "And he sure was right!"

Peyton Ramsey stabilized the position, helping the Wildcats improve from 3-9 to 7-2 in the COVID-shortened season.

"Some folks' DNA is to be uber hands-on," Fitzgerald says. "Other dads are more like the bumpers in bumper bowling. That's how I approach it with my son, Ryan. I just want to be a bumper for him. I want to give him the latitude to learn and grow."

Fitzgerald himself is now a Quarterback Dad. Ryan, his middle son, started in the fall of 2021 for Loyola Academy's freshman team and got called up to the varsity for the playoffs as a backup. Big brother Jack caught 25 passes as a junior tight end at Loyola. The youngest Fitzgerald, 13-year-old Brendan, plays fullback and defensive end for his North Shore Trevians youth team.

Pat is old school, a huge advocate of playing multiple sports and a steadfast believer that social media is a waste of time.

On playing a range of sports, he says: "Ryan plays basketball and baseball. Our guys played hockey, volleyball. Our guys do everything, man. Just have fun. There's huge value in that — muscle memory, developing different skills and techniques."

As the sons of a Big Ten head coach playing at a prominent high school near a huge city, Fitzgerald's kids don't need the social media buzz. But I asked Fitzgerald if he agrees with those parents who say they use Twitter to get their kids noticed and invited to camps.

"No," he says. "Not at all. (At Northwestern) we're going to work through the high school coaches to figure out who these kids are. We are not going to work through what their parents put on social media. We want an unbiased source. If the parents want to get their kid's quote-unquote 'brand' out there, feel free. But at what point does it become a pain in the neck?"

Fitzgerald has no issues with parents who hire a private quarterback tutor, calling it "an amazing boutique industry."

After all, he is one of those parents.

Ryan Fitzgerald works with Persa, who completed a Big Ten-record 73.5% of his passes in 2010. He clearly slipped in 2011, completing 73.4%.

"Sure, Danny knows the fundamentals and mechanics, but it's more of what Danny exuded when he played for us," Fitzgerald says. "The mental makeup, the football knowledge, the football IQ. If Ryan was getting ready to play tight end or linebacker, Dad would have some expertise for him. At the quarterback position, there's nobody I trust more than Danny Persa."

Persa works full-time at Coldwell Banker Real Estate in Chicago. His side gig is quarterback training, something that was not really available while growing up in Bethlehem, Pa. He recalls having maybe one session with the father of Dan Kendra, a high school All-American who played at Florida State.

Dan Persa Sr. was an enthusiastic sports dad ... but not a quarterback. So he handed off his son to his high school coaches and, eventually, Fitzgerald's staff.

"My dad taught me how to throw, but that's where the tutelage ended," Persa says. "I got taught by others, and I think it's better that way. It prepares you for the real world. You've got to earn everything and build relationships. Trust people."

Persa backed up a pair of terrific college quarterbacks: C.J. Bacher and Kafka. In his first three seasons, Persa attempted just 34 passes.

"At Northwestern there were times my dad wondered why I wasn't playing," Persa says. "I'm sure he said stuff to (offensive coordinator Mick) McCall every now and then, but he wasn't calling him every day — not to my knowledge anyway. For most kids it's beneficial to be coached by people you don't know. Have your dad in the background."

Persa waited his turn and became a two-time captain, two-time team MVP and the first-team All-Big Ten quarterback in 2010. He's grateful he didn't play in an era of transfer portals and extreme impatience, saying he couldn't have envisioned leaving his friends at Northwestern and starting over.

Persa tutors a handful of high school-aged quarterbacks around Chicago. With younger kids who are still developing physically, he says, "one day they can throw it 20 yards and the next day 40. Makes it kind of fun. (Quarterbacking) has a lot of unnatural movement. You have to learn the fundamentals to harness your athletic ability."

Fitzgerald, he says, is a great Quarterback Dad because he "doesn't get involved too much. Not much positive or negative. He might say, 'Hey, Ryan, don't be so hard on yourself' or add some color."

That's consistent with the Fitzgerald mantra regarding Quarterback Dads. In simplest terms, let your kid's coach, coach.

"The great (Quarterback Dads)," Fitzgerald says, "support their child and say: Listen to your coaches, be a great teammate and leader and go play ball. If you're meant to win the job, you will. If not, either find a way to play another position or be a great No. 2 and learn how to hold (on kicks)."

CHAPTER 20

THE QUARTERBACK DAD NO LONGER

Phil Rochelle needs to appear in a Netflix series. Check that. He needs his own Netflix series.

"Listen to me, playa," he says. "I used to rap against Ice-T. We was on some fly-ass shit!"

Phil is from a rough part of Los Angeles but calls it Hollywood. He believes it's important for football players to entertain and essential for them to build a brand. His son already has a cool name: Rashad Rochelle. But he goes by "Train."

Why?

"When he was in the womb at like 4-5 months, we had a doctor's visit," Phil recalls. "They did the ultrasound. The doctor said his heartbeat is so fast, it sounds like a train coming across the tracks. I said: If it's a boy, his nickname will be Train."

When Phil felt Train wasn't getting enough publicity, he researched football recruiting analysts and discovered Allen Trieu of 247Sports. "We're looking for some exposure," he texted Trieu. "My son is gonna be the bomb!"

Train was 6 at the time.

Phil sent pictures of his little tyke scoring touchdowns and making layups. And that's not it. Trieu received photos of Train fishing, playing with Legos and doing his homework.

"I shot my shot," Phil says. "I don't give a f**k who you are or who you think you are; everybody needs a relationship! I know that from Hollywood."

Even among obsessive Quarterback Dads, Trieu says, Rochelle "might be top of the mountain."

He's definitely over the top. But he's also endearing. And entertaining. Our 60-minute phone interview was loaded with fly-ass shit.

"I was born in Chicago," Phil says. "Cook County, East 87th and Avalon. Moved to L.A. at 10. My old man had family out there. I thought I was Magic Johnson, playa. Sheee-it. I couldn't be Kareem. Wasn't 7 feet. Still had to walk the block, you know what I'm saying?"

Not really.

But I wanted to hear more.

Phil played football at Culver City High School, an option quarterback aspiring to be the next Jamelle Holieway. Culver City teammate Carnell Lake steered clear of the gangs, ended up playing at UCLA and made five Pro Bowls with the Steelers and Jaguars. Phil could not dodge trouble. He went to the University of Tulsa to play ball but lasted about as long as one of Holieway's scampers to the end zone at Oklahoma.

"I wasn't focused," Phil says. "So I'm raising my son to realize the opportunity he has."

Mission accomplished. Start with Train's high school career, which concluded in breathtaking fashion. His Springfield team in central Illinois gave up 72 points to Rock Island. But that's cool considering his crew scored a Class 6A playoff-record 94 points. Train accounted for nine touchdowns in the win, throwing for six (9-for-16, 263 yards) and rushing for three (184 yards). Again, this was a playoff game. Springfield hadn't won a postseason game in 11 years. Hope there was supplemental oxygen on the sidelines.

Springfield lost the next week to Lemont despite Train's 146 passing yards, 92 rushing yards and 96-yard kickoff return. That marked a major transition for Train, a four-year starter at quarterback.

A year earlier, Phil still viewed Train as a quarterback in the mold of Kyler Murray or Russell Wilson. He raved of his son: "He has a cannon arm and he can cut the field in half in five seconds."

Phil says Duke offered Train as a quarterback, as did Central Michigan, Illinois State, Western Illinois and Eastern Illinois. But the Big Ten schools that were in on Train, including Purdue and Illinois, viewed him as a receiver. After all, Train is 5-11, 165 pounds with blinding speed (sub-4.5) and a broad jump (11 feet, 1 inches) that compares favorably to the NFL's top playmakers.

A "freakazoid of an athlete," Trieu says.

Rutgers did a superior job in its recruitment and got rewarded with a commitment. Train enrolled early, at age 17, and arrived on the New Jersey campus in January 2022. Rutgers sent so many handwritten letters, "I could wallpaper my son's room with them," Phil says.

"We considered Duke," he says, "but Rutgers threw the farm at us and we are not gonna turn down a free farm, if you know what I'm saying. The Rutgers coaches answered my tough questions, where others said, 'We'll cross that bridge when we get there.'"

Other recruiters spoke in generalities about what Train would need to do to play as a freshman. Rutgers presented a plan, which focuses on beefing up his frame.

"I can't force him to eat," Phil says, "but at Rutgers when they say, 'Eat,' you eat. If they say, 'Hit these weights,' you hit these weights."

And they helped win over Phil by, as he puts it, "making me feel like I could be myself."

"When I came to visit, they had Coors Light for me," he says. "They put that in my hotel room. That's the kind of shit we talked about! They didn't make me feel like I was doing anything wrong. If I did that at Duke, they'd probably say: Is his dad an alcoholic?"

Train is an only child and has been Phil's pet project from the moment he transitioned from dribbling milk to a Nerf basketball.

"I used to spend a lot of time with him from when he was 2 years old, when shorties can really run," Phil says. "We incorporated football into play time. Most parents play with puzzles or sandboxes. Me and Train used to play football where he'd run and I'd tackle or trip him. He'd laugh and we'd go at it again!"

Phil says that as Train aged, he found baseball boring "but was cold-blooded in hoops. They compared him to Paul Pierce. He said: 'Dad, what you think?' I told him: 'You're not gonna be 6-8. If I was you, I'd focus on football.'"

Plus, as Phil put it: "I know a lot about football, bro. A lot."

At least enough to be dangerous. Phil always had an opinion on how Train should be coached.

Train started playing at age 5 — against 6-year-olds. The family opted to live in Springfield because Phil's wife, Phyllis, works for the state as an accountant. (Phil is a city foreman.) They're middle class, with an in-ground pool in a neighborhood with doctors and lawyers.

"I tease him all the time about that," Phil says. "I don't have a college degree. I'm a hustler, motherf**ker."

Springfield is Illinois' state capital, and Phil says even youth football can get weighed down by politics. He "had it out with one coach" who opted to start his son at quarterback rather than Train.

"Whenever his son played, we didn't do shit. With my son in, we started winning," he says. "We had words, bro."

Phil has been sending video clips to coaches since Train was in sixth grade, making the old man something of a runaway train. He was a bit more restrained as Train rose through the youth football ranks, declining to personally coach him.

Phil said Train's coaches wanted him around the team "because of my personality; everybody knew I had a shot to play in the NFL.

I was the guy saying: 'Look, man, you ain't gonna f**k over my son.' I was never the head coach or a position coach, but maybe I was the equipment guy. I was helping out, bringing out pizza after the game."

Central Michigan offered Train a scholarship after his sophomore season. Purdue, Duke, Illinois and Rutgers followed in the late summer and fall. But some coaches declined out of concern over Train's size or, to be frank, Phil's hustle game.

"Don't waste another minute on him," one Big Ten coach told his staff. "I don't care if the kid is Johnny Unitas."

He's closer to Johnny Football.

Johnny Manziel was an athletic marvel, a slight 6-footer who made the finger-rubbing money sign his signature celebration.

Although his son got plenty of love from college recruiters and ended up as the 15th-ranked player in Illinois, Phil remains displeased that he was labeled a three-star recruit. He wanted a fourth star to raise Train's profile, likening it to more people noticing a Mercedes that is "washed and waxed."

While Train focuses on the X's and O's, his father ponders three other letters: NIL — as in name, image and likeness. College athletes can now profit off their names, whether that be endorsing products, signing autographs or offering personal training. Rutgers had a logo ready for Train's arrival on campus.

The marketplace will be a challenge, though, considering Rutgers has one of the smallest fan bases in the Big Ten, plays in the shadow of the Jets and Giants and hasn't had a winning season since 2014.

And another thing: Train is no longer a quarterback. Phil says he's fine with becoming a Wide Receiver Dad.

"I told Train when he was little: 'Listen, man, the reason you're playing quarterback is so college coaches can see the ball in your hands at all times.' I was more set on marketing his athleticism and decision-making versus him being a pure quarterback. It's about playing football, not about playing a position.

"Plus there's less stress as a receiver. He just has his job to do —
run those routes and block. He doesn't have to scream at a lineman
who missed a block or tell a receiver: Hey, that was supposed to be a
5-yard out!"

The top-of-the-mountain dad knows that in Hollywood, supporting actors get paid too.

"Train loves his nickname," Phil says. "His mom calls him Rashad,
of course. But his coaches, his teachers, his friends, they all call him
Train. Rashad Rochelle sounds good too. Goes together like bacon
and eggs. Rashad Rochelle ... Big Ten Freshman of the Year!"

CHAPTER 21

THE MOVIE STAR QUARTERBACK DAD

The man who taught himself to throw a spiral is now a human instruction manual.

"I had nothing," Kurt Warner says. "And I had nobody to teach me anything about the game."

Kurt Warner could have used Kurt Warner. Then again, he did OK on his own.

Warner orchestrated "The Greatest Show on Turf" for the St. Louis Rams from 1999-2001. He completed 40 passes in a single game. He threw for a then-record 414 yards in Super Bowl XXXIV against the Titans. And the ultimate: In a 2000 playoff victory over the Packers, he had more touchdown passes (five) than incompletions (four).

Even the major motion picture on his life, "American Underdog," was well-received after its Christmas 2021 release.

Warner got by on a combination of athleticism and determination. Or maybe it was stubbornness. Football kept telling him to scram, get lost.

He was a superb high school quarterback in Burlington, Iowa, but coaches from the two in-state Power Five schools didn't even call. He went to Northern Iowa on a partial scholarship and sat on the bench for the better part of four seasons. He lit it up as a senior, winning Gateway Conference Player of the Year, but did not get drafted. The Packers took a look, yawned and released him.

Take the hint, kid.

Warner refused. He stocked shelves at a Hy-Vee grocery store for $5.50 an hour and signed with the Iowa Barnstormers of the Arena Football League. He put up huge numbers in 1995. And '96. And '97. Then he hit Amsterdam for a stint in NFL Europe. The Rams picked him up but didn't play him. In 1998, he completed 4 of 11 passes — for the season.

Hey, kid, what did we tell you?

But during a preseason game in 1999, Trent Green took a brutal hit and blew out his knee. Coach Dick Vermeil openly cried before handing the ball to Warner, who led the NFL in completion percentage at 65.1%. He repeated the next season (67.7%) and the next (68.7%). The Rams went 35-8 during that stretch. Remarkably, Warner is the last NFL player to win both MVP and Super Bowl MVP in the same season.

Now he's eager — no, determined — no, hell-bent — to share what he knows. That's why he founded the website QBConfidential. com, which pledges to "build better players, smarter coaches and more informed fans."

It's also why he invited Donovan Dooley and a group of young quarterbacks to his home in spring 2021 (Chapter 1) for a two-day summit.

"Anybody who's passionate about it and wants to learn, call me," he says. "Even NFL quarterbacks. I say call me, and nobody ever does. I'm here. That's how Coach Dooley and I got hooked up. He reached out on Twitter and asked: 'Can you help me? I want to fly some guys out.' I said: 'Sure, come on, let's do it.'

"Too many coaches don't look to find out more. And that's frustrating. That's why when you have Coach Dooley saying, 'I want to understand it better' ... great, I'll teach you so then you can teach the next generation, and the future of the game will be in better shape."

Warner runs the group of 11 quarterbacks and 11 receivers through two hours of morning drills at his magnificent compound in

Scottsdale, Ariz. After he asks them to gather, they form a semicircle. Several dads approach with recording devices, using their phones or iPads to capture every syllable falling from Warner's lips.

"If anybody wants to learn the game, I'm here all day," he says. "It's like money. The older I get, the more I want to share it. So if I can help anybody to get better — coaching or playing — I'm all in. The details of the game fascinate me."

He asks the players: "How special are you? Can you be Patrick Mahomes? Can you be Aaron Rodgers? Maybe a couple of you can. I couldn't. I had no chance to be that guy. When I retired, I was one of the most accurate quarterbacks in NFL history. Why? Because I had good technique.

"You guys are so far ahead of the game because you're out here with somebody trying to teach you how to play the position. I had nobody. They put a ball in my hand and I had to learn as I go. You guys are ahead of the game with what you have access to, but I'm gonna say this: How good you want to be is up to you. You guys have the tools."

A young quarterback with Warner's DNA kneels to his right. Elijah Warner, who goes by EJ, leans on a football and listens in. And then Warner calls him out. It isn't brutal, but it's enough to irk him.

"Don't wait to be coached," Warner tells the group. "Learn how to play the position so you can go out in your backyard and get better without having to say: 'Coach, can you come to my house and watch everything I do?' EJ wants (me) to do that all the time. 'Dad, tell me what I did wrong every single play.'"

And with that, EJ raises his palms as if to ask: How did I get dragged into this?

"It's hard sometimes," EJ says later off to the side, "because he pushes me more than other kids. There's some arguing and there's stuff I have to balance. But I mean, I love it. I take everything he teaches me (and I incorporate) it into my game, so it's awesome."

As the son of a legendary quarterback, one determined to teach proper mechanics and with the resources to construct a football field in his backyard, EJ has it great.

And as the son of a legendary quarterback, one determined to teach proper mechanics and with the resources to construct a football field in his backyard, EJ has it rough.

You get the dichotomy, right? Every aspiring quarterback would like to be in EJ's shoes. Until they'd have to dodge a blitz. Or get taunted by fans.

Having WARNER on the back of your jersey while playing high school football in Arizona must be like walking to a movie set as Colin Hanks. To whom much is given …

"My wife and I tell our kids: 'You were born into this. You didn't ask for it,'" Kurt says. "There is a stigma, and I think that's one of the reasons why Kade never played quarterback. He almost sabotaged it: 'Everybody expects me to play quarterback. I'm not playing quarterback. I don't want that pressure. I don't want to have to walk in his footsteps.'"

Indeed, EJ's big brother Kade opted to play receiver. He made 30 catches for Nebraska from 2018-20 before transferring to Kansas State, where he caught 14 balls for 166 yards last season.

"One of the reasons I think he went to the Midwest was to get out of Arizona: I'll get away from Dad and I'm going to just write my own story," Kurt says.

And then, in the next breath, a glimpse of why.

"EJ is so much better than I was at his age," Kurt says. "I mean, it's not even close."

Kurt is a fierce advocate of EJ's. And that, of course, is a beautiful thing. In the spring of 2020, he tweeted out a four-minute video of one of EJ's workouts and wrote: "Too many (colleges) missing on @ elijah13warner — but it's all good, bc as I know, all it takes is 1 … the question is who's it going to be? Who's getting a steal?"

Asked if he can evaluate EJ in an unbiased way, Kurt replies: "I think I'm very realistic. I don't think I sugarcoat it. I know what goes into the position. I'm probably overly critical because I know what he's capable of and what I want him to be. I don't assess him as a dad; I assess him as a quarterback. At the same time it's my reputation too. I don't want anyone to say: 'This is a biased dad who thinks his son is great.' If I say my son is great and he turns out to be awful, then it is what it is.

"Also you'll notice. I never post anything without video to go with it. When I'm on the NFL Network, I don't just say a quarterback is doing something. I like to show it so I have something to back it up. When I post on EJ, it's posted with video. If you doubt me, look, tell me this guy can't play."

Within weeks of Warner declaring that, his viewpoint was validated. Several FBS schools offered scholarships, including Colorado State.

"A Warner as a Ram," Kurt wrote on Twitter, "has a nice ring to it!!!"

In the end, EJ Warner chose a different animal, an Owl. In January he tweeted an image of himself in a cherry-colored jersey and helmet: "100% committed to Temple University!!!"

CHAPTER 22

HEY, QUARTERBACK DADS, SEEK THERAPY

Robert Jamerson has seen it all. And heard it all.

He's the CEO of Detroit's Police Athletic League (PAL), which provides year-round programming to thousands of kids in 11 sports, from golf to cheer to T-ball to, of course, football. PAL's stated mission is "Helping Youth Find Their Greatness," and parents and guardians can register kids to play flag football at age 5 and tackle at 7.

Its football alumni include NFL standouts Brandon Graham (Eagles), Jordan Lewis (Cowboys), Desmond King (Texans) and Allen Robinson (Bears). Donovan Dooley never made the pros, but he thrived in the program. Jamerson coached him and became his mentor, teaching him a bevy of life lessons:

Be a continuous learner.

Align with people who are good at what they do.

Work while you sleep. The body can go only so far, but the mind operates continuously.

Create additional revenue streams.

That final tip resulted in Dooley's creating Quarterback University and led to his seeking a writing partner and author for "Quarterback Dads." Dooley knew he had a story to share after being party to all the cringeworthy fathers who could not get out of their own way. Or their son's way. Or the way of the quarterback trainer they hired.

153

Jamerson encouraged Dooley to get the word out after working with parents and players for decades at PAL, where he also has served as a coach and consultant. (His day job is in pharmaceuticals; he's an MBA who spent 17 years at Pfizer in a variety of capacities, including strategic planning and mental health.)

One of his favorite sayings is this: "You manage things. You lead people."

Quarterbacks need to lead. Everyone knows this. But Jamerson is uniquely qualified to make this next observation: Quarterback Dads need to be led. He sees it time and time again with promising prospects who go through the PAL program.

"I think of it as training," Jamerson says. "There should be a training for Quarterback Dads. A lot of them don't know what they're getting into. It's a humbling role because they're putting their kid out there when, mentally, he may not be ready to be exposed to the reality and harshness of the world. Quarterbacks are evaluated at an age where it's just not fair. They miss out on an opportunity to just go out, have fun and be a kid."

As rough as it can be for the player, it can be worse for the dad.

Jamerson has sat in the stands at games with dads who are so oblivious to the parents around them, they holler: "Get that kid out of there! What the heck is he doing?!"

How should the Quarterback Dad respond? Ignore the offending parent ... or threaten to punch his lights out? Similar incidents occur at camps, where parents sometimes actively root against quarterbacks so their son will earn a higher ranking.

More stressful situations can emerge in relation to playing time. Is your son second string because the coach is playing the son of the principal? If you're the backup, should you sit and wait your turn — or transfer? Should you be brutally honest with your son after a poor performance — or relentlessly positive and leave the negative stuff to his coaches?

"Being a Quarterback Dad can be the cause of all sorts of challenges in the household, even divorce," Jamerson says. "Just sitting with all the other parents can be draining."

Jamerson's advice?

"Seek therapy," he says.

He's not kidding.

"I'm surprised there's not a therapist who specializes in Quarterback Dads," he says. "It's already difficult enough for dads to interact with their own son. You'll want to have counseling."

Perhaps that's a dim view, but it results from decades of player-dad observations.

Should fathers coach their own kids?

That's a tricky one, Jamerson says. It might work in the younger years, but is the father able to trade in his metaphorical whistle for a dad cap when he walks through the front door? If not, don't even try it. And even if so, be wary.

"A lot of times, dads are either too hard or too enabling; they need to find the sweet spot," Jamerson says. "Quarterbacks have to be their own worst critics — and cannot get too high or too low. And if the dad can't switch hats when he gets home, burnout can occur. The kid has to be able to distance himself (from football) and get nurtured. There needs to be a balance."

Jamerson played quarterback at St. Martin de Porres, helping the all-Black Catholic high school in Detroit win a state title in 1989. Greg Carter, a towering figure on the Detroit prep sports scene, helped coach that team under Ron Thompson. Carter became head coach in 1994 after Thompson died.

Seven years later, he fielded a team with an undersized starting quarterback. Dooley was 5-foot-10 but also skilled, confident and possessing an immeasurable love for football and the nuances of the quarterback position. And he was tough. His parents, Ella and William Sr., chose his name because Donovan means "warrior" or "strong fighter" in Celtic.

He had to be strong mentally to thrive in a tough-love household that reflected the times. William Sr. never played organized football, but he knew the game as the older brother of an all-state linebacker nicknamed "Snookie" Dooley.

"If I had a good game, my dad would never tell me," Dooley says. "If I threw for one touchdown pass, it should have been two. Two, it should have been three. He'd tell me all the things I did wrong. What I took away from that is never be complacent."

William Sr. and Snookie grew up in the Jeffries Housing Projects, a series of high-rises that became a magnet for crime and violence in the '80s. William Sr., Donovan says, was a "hoodlum" growing up but eventually reformed thanks to the love and dedication of Ella. They grew up across the way and met as preteens.

William Sr. didn't graduate from high school with his class but earned a GED, which stood for "Good enough, dummy," he joked.

He worked in a hospital for more than 40 years, and Donovan says his father did not miss a single day during a 28-year stretch. Vacations were nonexistent. Snookie, meanwhile, fell adrift and became an alcoholic and drug addict. He lived on the streets.

Those examples were seared into Donovan's mind. Work ethic meant everything.

Though his father did not shower him with love, "he surrounded me with good people. When I was playing youth football, he was absolutely a Quarterback Dad. But by the time I got to high school, he wasn't trying to inject himself into a scheme or play call."

Carter began coaching at St. Martin de Porres in 1978 and was inducted into the Michigan High School Football Coaches Association Hall of Fame in 2020. He remains a key figure on the Detroit sports scene, now the head coach at Oak Park High School.

"He's a man of character, a man of his word, no nonsense," Dooley says. "If he said, 'You're out two quarters,' it damn sure would be two. He was very blunt with me, saying, 'Keep working' and 'What are you gonna do, quit?'"

Dooley starred on the JV team as a sophomore, but Carter, stressing seniority, left him on the bench his junior year. Every morning Dooley would stop by the coach's office to tease him, saying: "You know I should be starting, right?"

The response: Get your ass to class, boy!

Jamerson, when returning to his alma mater to watch practices and games, would notice some friction between Carter and Dooley. He provided a bridge between the two, serving as a "Phil Jackson" sounding board for a frustrated player and an old-school coach.

"Donovan never had prototypical size," Jamerson says, "but he had heart and belief in himself."

Both Dooley and Jamerson have September birthdays that make them Virgos. Dooley does not believe in astrology, but Jamerson is a loyal subscriber. He says it's a factor in their bond.

"September kids are very analytical and observant — and can be sensitive," he says. "When Donovan is coaching people, it's bigger than the X's and O's. He has empathy for kids and applies his own experience for how a Quarterback Dad should interact with his son."

Just as Jamerson served as a buffer between Dooley and Carter, Dooley tries to smooth the friction between a quarterback and his dad. Especially with the fathers who qualify as "The Helicopter Dad" or "The Demonstrator Dad," Dooley tries to open or strengthen the lines of communication.

"A leader cannot have one type of approach after a coach or teammate has demoralized him," Jamerson said. "(Even Bill) Belichick understands the love language and that not everyone should be treated the same.

"Donovan relates to the kids and connects with them on a personal standpoint. He knows the anxiety they're under, the pressure the parents knowingly or unknowingly put on them. Donovan will ask the kid: You're making all the throws here (in drills). What's the difference when you put the pads on or when the lights come on?"

Jamerson expressed the same kind of empathy when Dooley bristled under Carter's tight watch. Carter ran a veer system that typically allowed for fewer than a dozen pass attempts a game. Dooley's only audible at the line was to alter a running play — from the left to the right or vice versa.

Dooley jokes about how Carter would impress the players' parents by putting his arm around them as they walked to the sideline.

"The parents never knew he was cussing us out," Dooley says with a laugh. "It looked like he was consoling us, but he'd be giving us 'the real' under his breath: 'Make that damn play or I will sit your ass down.'"

Dooley helped deliver one of the four state titles Carter won as head coach at St. Martin de Porres. The Division 7 championship game was played at the Pontiac Silverdome, the former home of the Lions. Dooley can remember intricate details of the game, even though he's sure he suffered a concussion at the hands of the Cassleman brothers, Bill and Jim, of Muskegon Central Catholic.

"They tagged my ass," he says.

Dooley was so woozy after getting sacked, he went under center. And then into the shotgun. And then under center. Back and forth he went before the ball was even snapped. But he remained in the game, rushing 12 times for 60 yards. He chuckles now upon seeing the rest of his line: 5 of 8 passing for 66 yards. The opposing quarterback went 2-for-3.

De Porres won 23-7.

"We didn't care about stats," Dooley says. "It was all about winning. How many times I threw the ball didn't cross my mind. Now I'd be asking the coach: 'What the hell is going on?'"

Dooley takes as much pride in that performance as he does in something his coach said during the broadcast.

"That kid," Carter said, "used to tell me every day that he should be starting."

CHAPTER 23

HUNDRED-DOLLAR HANDSHAKES

There was the time a Quarterback Dad handed Allen Trieu (pro-nounced "True") a folded-up $100 bill with these instructions: Take your wife to dinner. The time another sent a gift basket to Trieu's home. (It was unsigned, making the gesture even more useless.) And the topper — the time a Quarterback Dad offered to deliver Trieu's wife's baby for free in exchange for giving his kid two stars.

A mere two stars!

When was this?

"My son is 8 now," Trieu says.

Which is to say, Quarterback Dads have been crazy for a while now.

"And getting crazier," says Trieu, who analyzes Midwest recruiting for 247Sports.com. "The Quarterback Dad was the pioneer; now the dads at every other position are trying to be like them."

Dream, baby, dream.

You want the lowdown on quarterbacks, you ask the scouts. You want the nitty-gritty on Quarterback Dads, you ask the recruiting analysts.

Greg Biggins, also an analyst for 247Sports, focuses on recruiting in Southern California. That's an area that recently produced Alabama's Bryce Young and D.J. Uiagalelei, who took over as the starter at Clemson in 2021 after Trevor Lawrence went first in the NFL draft.

It's also a hotbed for wannabe quarterbacks and dads who want to be omnipresent.

"I've seen quarterbacks transfer three or four times in their high school career," Biggins says. "Nobody wants to sit the bench for even a year. Dads call and say: 'Hey, my kid has to play by his freshman year. Can you recommend some high schools?' I say: 'My advice, sir, is that I don't think your kid should play as a freshman. He is not emotionally ready. The emotional gap is too great. I've seen kids get ruined.'"

To which the dad replies: "No, my kid is mature. I just want to know a school where he can play."

And then Biggins supplies the dagger: "If he could (play), he would have been hit up 100 times by now."

The best Quarterback Dads, Biggins says, are like Craig Young. Biggins declared this months before Young's son, Bryce, became the first Crimson Tide quarterback to win the Heisman Trophy. Young was the top QB in the 2020 class, followed by Uiagalelei and another native Californian, C.J. Stroud, who threw for 3,862 yards at Ohio State in 2021.

As chronicled by The Ringer, Craig saw potential in Bryce at 6 months. After the little one caught a ball in his crib, Craig ran around the house screaming: "We got one! He's gonna be an athlete!"

But Craig and wife Julie never catered to Bryce. Perhaps that's why he never got a big head. Same as his old man.

"Bryce's dad is super humble," Biggins says. "He doesn't take shots at anyone. You never get the sense that it's all about football."

He tweets infrequently. And when he does, it's to promote his son — a new podcast episode, a high grade from Pro Football Focus or retweeting this quote from Bryce upon winning the Heisman: "Dreams do come true!!! Truly grateful for all those around me that made this night possible. Blessed beyond measure!"

Contrast that with the dads who use social media and message boards as forums for bitching and bullying. They rip their kid's coach, his offensive coordinator, the first-stringer who has the nerve to take their son's reps.

"I call them 'Daddy Ballers,'" Biggins says. "They are living vicariously through their kids. You read things and think: There's no way an adult would put that out there."

Like what?

" 'F' this coach; the system sucks. My kid should be playing over this kid," Biggins says. "There's such an entitlement. If my kid isn't playing, it's never because he's not good enough or someone is better. The system is bad, it's politics, the coach sucks, there's an agenda against him. Maybe parents always felt this way, but now they have vehicles to post it."

Tom Lemming can vouch for both ends of that. He has been grading recruits for so long, he dealt with Marv Marinovich.

"Marv was the extreme," Lemming says. "But a lot of fathers in that position live their lives through their sons. Sometimes the kid is the one running the family. The kid has been built up so much, he's the boss."

And some dads will do anything to please their sons. Lemming remembers the dad who offered the free use of his Florida beach house in exchange for a glowing report in Lemming's "Prep Football Report."

Quarterback Dads, Lemming says, have not evolved.

"They're almost exactly the same," he says. "What's changed is the platform to talk about their kids. Back then it was a telephone call to harass me. They would mail me VHS tapes. In the Elway/Marino era, a 16-millimeter. Then VHS tapes came in 1980-81.

"Fathers are always asking me to make calls to the college coaches. I tell them: When you're a great quarterback, there's no need for me to make calls for you."

Lemming drives tens of thousands of miles each year, crisscrossing the country to interview players and coaches for his nearly 300-page annual. The parents of quarterbacks are so eager to get their kid's name out, there are no hidden gems.

"I don't remember too many Michael Ohers at the quarterback position," says Lemming, who had a cameo role in the Sandra Bullock hit "The Blind Side."

Some dads have no patience. Or perspective.

"I get fathers calling me, and their son is 7 or 8 years old," he says. "I say: 'Please wait until he is going into high school.' Then the dads get upset."

The ultimate Quarterback Dad, in Lemming's estimation, was Archie Manning. The opposite of pushy. Handled everything with class. Both the intense Peyton and laid-back Eli thrived under his guidance. Of course when you're a Manning, there's no need to hunt for publicity. But in one case, there was a need for validation.

Lemming ranked Peyton as the No. 2 quarterback in the 1993 class. He gave top billing to another Louisianan, Josh Booty, who became the nation's first high school quarterback to throw for 10,000 yards. Booty chose baseball and a $1.6 million signing bonus from the Marlins before returning to football at LSU in his mid-20s.

In the early 2000s, Lemming ran into Peyton at the Manning Passing Academy. Peyton couldn't let the opportunity pass without asking: "Hey, Tom, how's your buddy Josh Booty doing?"

Like with Lemming, people take note of Trieu's arrival at quarterback camps. He stands out. As his 50,000-plus Twitter followers can see from his profile picture, he's Asian.

"It definitely hurts that I cannot blend into the crowd," he says. "One time I saw a bunch of people approaching another Asian guy. I looked and thought: I know exactly what is happening here!"

At the more elaborate camps, those held at high school fields with a press box, Trieu will climb to the top to try to get away and work on his evaluations. Inevitably, he will hear a tap on the press box window: "Hey, I just wanted to let you know that my kid is about to throw."

Trieu will sometimes invite the dad to sit next to him.

"My coworkers always tell me I'm too nice," he says. "Over the years I've gotten better at giving dads the honest spiel if their kid can't play at the level they think. I've tried to be professional, realistic and honest with them."

Steve Wiltfong, the director of recruiting for 247Sports, paints most Quarterback Dads in a positive light: "They're trying to do the best by their kid. They're personally invested, and that's a good thing, right? They want their kid to maximize his abilities. As a dad, I support that."

OK, free advice time.

I asked Wiltfong, Trieu and Biggins what they would tell Quarterback Dads who are open to listening. Here are some do's and don'ts:

DO: Use social media wisely

"I have four kids and tell them: Twitter is a cesspool," Biggins says. "But you kind of have to be on there so colleges can reach out to you. And you can hit up coaches. Control the narrative. Plus kids use it to break their own news."

Says Trieu of social media: "It's fine as long as you understand what it's there for and how to control it. Posting clips of throwing is good, especially during COVID (when high school games were canceled). But you better make sure the clips you're posting are quality. This is first exposure, and the coaches may never forget this view.

"If I was a parent of a kid getting recruited, I would buy a decent camera. Cellphone footage can be hard to see. If you're going to spend all this money on tutors and camps, spend a little money on a camera."

Wiltfong stresses common sense. If your kid is the starting quarterback at Don Bosco Prep in New Jersey or Cathedral High School in Indianapolis, go easy on the Twitter.

"If you live in the sticks," he says, "you might have to do a little more."

Above all else, do not drag down other players, especially those competing with your son. It's not only a terrible look but "a life lesson," Wiltfong says. "You get more bees with honey."

DO NOT: Seek publicity too early

Many Detroit football fans treated D'Wan Mathis and Sam Johnson III as celebrities before they even entered high school. Mathis could throw down windmill dunks at age 13 — and basketball wasn't even his best sport. Johnson fired the game-winning touchdown pass to lead his youth team, the Detroit Spartans, to a Police Athletic League title. The game was played at Ford Field, home of the Lions.

"They had the size, the athleticism, the parents," Dooley says. "Sam got exposure when he was 10, and D'Wan at 11. No one had ever seen inner-city quarterbacks like them. The community watched them play. You win championships, and you're an icon."

Akron coach Terry Bowden made Johnson the first eighth-grader in the state of Michigan to hold a college football offer. He had everything — size (6-3, 175), ability, acumen and determination. And two private trainers in Dooley and Quarterback University's Kevin Rogers, who told Rivals.com that Johnson "is 24/7 football ... on the field, in the weight room, in the classroom. His work ethic is crazy."

Michigan, Illinois and Iowa also made offers, but Johnson maintained his commitment to Boston College even after his main recruiter, offensive coordinator/quarterbacks coach Scot Loeffler, left Chestnut Hill to take over at Bowling Green.

Johnson never played a down at BC and announced on Twitter (under the handle @SJ_theFuture) in July 2020 that he would be transferring to Division II Shippensburg University. He didn't earn playing time there, either, registering no stats.

Mathis, meanwhile, originally committed to Iowa State. Then to Michigan State. Then Ohio State. After Urban Meyer stepped down, Mathis had another change of heart. He chose Georgia.

"That's the downside (of being highly rated)," Dooley says. "Kids go to college campuses and coaches are dangling carrots in front of their face and loving on them. It's like seeing a girl, and then you see a prettier one and then an even prettier one. You're falling into a trap, not realizing you're getting the used car salesman pitch.

"D'Wan then fell into the logo trap: I'm at Georgia, the top of the top. SEC. I'm a big fish. I'm considered the Next One."

He enrolled early and was named the starter in his redshirt freshman season in Athens. But Mathis completed just 8 of 17 throws with a red-zone interception in Georgia's 2020 opener against Arkansas and was benched in the second quarter.

"D'Wan is a freak of nature," says Dooley, who began training Mathis at age 9. "He can escape the pocket and make all the throws. But he's inconsistent with accuracy. He didn't dial into the X's and O's with me until it was late. He didn't find it important because he was able to overcome it with his athleticism."

Mathis lost his starting job and transferred to Temple, where coach Rod Carey named him the starter for the 2021 opener. But Mathis suffered a left leg injury in Week 1, another derailment that led him back to the transfer portal.

"Early attention sounds good," Trieu says, "but why not wait to allow the media to see you once you're as good as you can be? Sam and D'Wan got offers in the eighth grade, and I don't know that the early exposure was necessarily good for them. Neither asked for the scrutiny.

"It can hurt your development when you know every rep is being filmed. You're not going to be willing to try different things if you know that every throw will end up on Instagram."

The attention might be fun. And it might result in more offers. But in the end, what good does it do a young player?

"When you can do no wrong," Dooley says, "you get too many pats on the back and not enough kicks in the ass."

DO: Find a good QB trainer

At one time, only a handful existed. Now there might be a handful in your hometown.

"More and more come up every year," Trieu says. "It's harder to figure out who is legit and who is not."

Trieu recommends that parents get to know several private trainers before they settle on one. Watch them coach. If possible, talk to pupils and former clients. What kind of mechanics do they teach?

Trieu says Dooley "does a really good job. He vibes with the kids. They get along with him, so it's not a drag for them. And he puts the work in. My God, every time I talk to him, he's on a plane to another state. He has built up enough of a business where he could stand pat, but he's still learning."

Private trainers used to work only in the suburbs, Dooley says, catering to the parents who could afford them. Inner-city quarterbacks were at a huge disadvantage on the cerebral aspects of the position.

"Coaches would scream at them: 'Get it done!'" Dooley says. "But they were never told how to get it done."

Dooley is among those who brought top training to families of all income levels. Quarterback University has a program in which families that cannot afford tuition get sponsored by alumni, parents and affiliates. Those families in need must provide report cards and character progress reports for the student-athlete. One of the company mottos is "No quarterback left behind."

The proliferation of quarterback trainers, though, is also concerning. Which ones should be trusted?

"Anybody can make you sweat, but not everyone can make you better," Dooley likes to say. "You'll see guys go to Lifetime Fitness, get in shape, put on a tank top, watch some YouTube videos to steal some lingo and now they say they're a (quarterback) trainer. To the naïve parent, the dad who is an accountant and never played the sport, he's hearing hella word play, a whole bunch of terms that sound cool."

Darin Slack of The Quarterback Academy began offering quarterback coach certification in 2011. It did not catch on.

Biggins believes in private tutors because he has observed kids who he says had "no chance" to make it. "And then a year later, it's: Whoa, this kid has gotten better."

But be wary of the QB coaches who offer an endless array of compliments and rave about faux improvement. It's a business, after all, and trainers know what the people writing the checks (or clicking on Venmo) want to hear.

"If a trainer says everyone is gonna turn out good, then that's a damn lie," Dooley says. "It's like a piano class: Some will become musicians and some will just play in their house."

Dooley asks parents and aspiring quarterbacks their goals. He offers one promise: They will improve under his watch. He also offers brutal honesty. Sometimes a father will point to a 7-on-7 drill, beaming as his son rifles one picture-perfect pass after another.

"OK," Dooley will say. "But what's inside? I can't control his heartbeat."

DO NOT: Bombard recruiting analysts with calls/texts/DMs

As Trieu puts it: "The dad who is calling us every week during recruiting is the same one who will be (telling his son): 'Maybe you have to transfer.' And the same one asking the coach: 'Why did you run this play?'"

Biggins says they have a saying in the recruiting industry: "The crazier the dad, the cooler the kid."

He's reluctant to name names, but — cheat code — some examples have been documented in this book. We're talking about the dads who obsessively post their son's game film and stats.

"If you're on social media and posting more than your son does," Biggins says, "that's probably an issue."

169

CHAPTER 24

FROM QB LEGENDS TO FOOTBALL DADS

Greatness comes at a cost. But, no, this chapter won't contain a lecture. We won't instruct your teenage son to forgo the hangout with his friends in favor of a late-night trip to the gym.

Here's how the phrase applies to Warren Moon and Rick Neuheisel for our purposes: They do not consume their kids' sporting events the way you and I do. They can't. They're in the spotlight and know that any misstep will result in glares, whispers and perhaps an embarrassing video on social media.

"I can't be the rah-rah dad I want to," Moon says. "I never want to be *that* dad. I've trained myself to be low-key. It was the same when I played. My thing was to be the coolest player within all the chaos."

Worked pretty well. Moon is a remarkable American success story. He grew up in Los Angeles with six sisters. He avoided morning fights over the bathroom by showering the night before. He loved playing all sports but settled on football so he could work the rest of the year to support his family.

He attracted a big-name college, Washington, only after he grew past 6 feet and starred at West Los Angeles College. He led the Huskies to a 27-20 upset win over Michigan in the 1978 Rose Bowl but still felt NFL teams would not give him a legitimate shot at quarterback. So he signed with the CFL's Edmonton Eskimos.

His team won five consecutive Grey Cups and he became the first professional quarterback to throw for 5,000 yards in a season. Still, NFL teams mostly yawned. We know why, and it had nothing to do with his arm, which was elite.

As Moon explained in a 2017 piece by Jason Reid in The Undefeated, NFL talent evaluators felt African-Americans didn't have what it took to play "the thinking positions down the middle — quarterback, center and middle linebacker."

Disgusting.

Moon proved them wrong, earning nine trips to the Pro Bowl and a bust in Canton, Ohio. He has dabbled in private quarterback training, teaming with the acclaimed George Whitfield to tutor Cam Newton and Andrew Luck.

Moon has been a volleyball dad to daughters Blair and Chelsea and a football father — though not a Quarterback Dad — to three sons, including Joshua and Jeffrey.

"They did not want anything to do with being a quarterback," Moon says. "After watching me, they knew what they'd have to deal with. They wanted to play receiver."

His youngest, Ryken, is a talented Class of 2025 prospect in Bellevue, Wash., who already has been offered by Arizona. He, too, would rather catch passes than throw them.

"He wears my arm out," Warren says.

Moon never experienced the joy of seeing his own father in the stands. Warren does have memories of the two playing catch in the front yard, but Harold Moon was an alcoholic who died awaiting a liver transplant when Warren was 7. His mom, Pat, signed him up for Boy Scouts and Pop Warner football as a way for Warren to make friends and find male role models.

When Warren attends Ryken's games, he's careful not to cause a fuss. He's likely to set up a lawn chair at the far corner of the field. He wants the family members of other players to focus on the game rather than hunt him down for a picture or autograph.

And you will never hear Moon hassle a ref.

"I've seen too many dads get warned to keep it down — or not allowed back," he says. "It's amazing how parents can live their lives through their kids because they weren't successful (in sports). Dude, this is a Little League baseball game and you're arguing over a strike or ball? C'mon, don't look ignorant in front of your kids."

Six years after Moon delivered a Rose Bowl victory for the Pac-8, Neuheisel matched him. He completed 22 of 32 passes for UCLA in the Bruins' 45-9 throttling of Illinois. For that the blond quarterback was named Rose Bowl Offensive MVP.

The parallels don't end in Pasadena. Neuheisel, a longtime Quarterback Dad, made that perfectly clear when asked for his No. 1 piece of advice.

"When you go to the games, make sure you sit where no one can hear you," he says. "Go to a far corner of the stands, somewhere where you can say something about the coach or the refs and not be admonished."

Like Moon, Neuheisel grew up with sisters but no brother. His father, Dick, whose basketball career was curtailed by injury, obsessed over sports. He took young Rick to Lambeau Field and then, after the family moved to Arizona, to Phoenix Suns games and sporting events at Arizona State, where he taught law. Dick would have him recite the New York Knicks' championship starting five to friends.

"From the first day I can remember, we were throwing the ball in the backyard," Rick says. "I definitely was led to the altar."

Rick was 27 when the SI story on Todd Marinovich came out. He recalls thinking that Todd's father "was trying to manufacture the perfect quarterback, like Lee Majors and 'The Six Million Dollar Man.' Everything was being engineered, and he wasn't allowed to eat Big

Macs. I would have never survived doing that. I thought that when he got to (USC's) campus, there would be a rebellion."

Marinovich's uprising did not come soon enough as far as UCLA was concerned. In 1990, Neuheisel was in his third season as a full-time Bruins assistant. As he recalls, "Todd played and the Trojans beat us 45-42."

Beyond the similar SoCal ties, about the only parallel between the Marinovich and Neuheisel paths was the father's unyielding belief in his son. Dick Neuheisel served as the manager of Rick's Little League teams and the coach of his basketball teams. Rick played the premier positions: pitcher/shortstop and point guard. But in football, he played receiver.

That changed in eighth grade when his team's starting quarterback came down with Valley fever, an infection not uncommon in the Southwest.

"Unbeknownst to me," Rick says, "my dad went to the coach and said: 'My son is your quarterback. Don't take my word for it. Put him in and see what you think.' I'd always been the guy catching the passes. I could throw it, but I wasn't hell-bent on being a quarterback. Then I realized how fun it was."

In his first game, Rick completed 11 of 12 passes.

Rick could have played at Princeton. Navy and Division I-AA programs such as Weber State were also interested in the 6-1, 180-pound prospect. But Rick walked on at UCLA, seeking the spotlight. Instead he found an occasional — and unsatisfying — role on special teams while not getting a single practice rep at quarterback in his first two seasons.

Dozens of times, he called home and told his father he wanted to transfer. Dozens of times, his father told him: Relax, stay patient and see how it goes.

Neuheisel finally got the chance to start during his fifth season. Brimming with confidence, if not ability, he once had this exchange, according to Sports Illustrated, with offensive coordinator Homer Smith.

Smith: "Do you think you can complete 80 percent of your passes in a 7-on-7 drill?"

Neuheisel: "Eighty percent if you call the plays. Ninety percent if I call them."

Neuheisel maxed out his college career, losing and then regaining his starting spot in his final season after an injury to Steve Bono. He had a 25-for-27 passing performance against Washington, led UCLA to the Pac-10 title and overcame food poisoning to fire four touchdown passes in the Rose Bowl. He played briefly in the USFL before assuming the role he was born to do — coach.

He became head coach at Colorado at age 34, the second-youngest in Division I-A football. He went 33-14 and 3-0 in bowl games before leaving for Washington, where he became one of five coaches in the nation to make $1 million. He later returned to his alma mater for a four-year stretch that ended with a 21-29 record and a firing.

Along the way he experienced every type of Quarterback Dad. The best ones, he says, knew football but did not attempt to intervene. Two examples are the fathers of Marques Tuiasosopo, who led Washington to a Rose Bowl victory over Purdue and Drew Brees, and Koy Detmer, who had a 3,000-yard passing season at Colorado. Hubert "Sonny" Detmer was himself a coach, mainly at Texas high schools.

"He was a fanatic but stayed totally clear," Rick says. "When he called it was to say: 'Hey, Coach, I like what you did there (on a certain play).' It was coach to coach. Marques' dad, Manu, played D-line (in the NFL) and knew that toughness was a big part of the game."

And the bad ones?

"There were disagreements," Rick says. "I'd say: You're here because you love your son and you *should* be his biggest fan. But you have to realize it would be ridiculous for me to keep him down if I thought he was my best quarterback. As much as you disagree, you have to understand I'm doing what I think is best.

"At least I tried. There were quarterbacks who packed up and left."

More than 1,600 scholarship players entered the NCAA transfer portal after the 2020 season. Neuheisel understands the desire to seek greener pastures, but he wouldn't mind reminding players and parents about his story and extreme patience, which resulted in a happy ending — leaving Rose Bowl tickets for his family.

"It's a little disconcerting that so many youngsters and emotional parents want to press the eject button," he says. "There are not (1,600) landing spots."

I put Neuheisel on my must-interview list after reading his take on Quarterback Dads in Bruce Feldman's fascinating 2014 book, "The QB: The Making of Modern Quarterbacks."

As Neuheisel put it to Feldman: "The QB dads are like nomads in the desert. If you tell 'em there's water, they're gonna drink it. They want their sons so badly to have the instruction, so if you have any sales ability at all, you can make them believe they have to know what you know. All you have to do is tell 'em: He's got *it*. And they'll keep spending. And spending. And spending."

Have Quarterback Dads gotten even crazier since he delivered that line?

"Probably, because of the growth of 7-on-7s and the quarterback gurus," he replies. "The (tutors) are well-intended guys, but they're also business guys. To run a business, you're going to say what (fathers) want to hear and create aspirations and expectations for guys who should not have them. Look, there is nothing wrong with dreaming. I walked on and dreamt about becoming a starter. But there's also a time to say: Go play at this level (FCS, Division II or III) and enjoy the heck out of it."

Neuheisel defines a Quarterback Dad as one "who goes to every game and has stars in his eyes when he talks about his boy. That's a great thing, but when they become critical of anyone who constructively coaches their kid, it's to his detriment."

That goes beyond being a hovering helicopter parent. To borrow a line from Northwestern coach Pat Fitzgerald, they become a snowplow parent — clearing out any hurdles so the journey down the mountain will be as smooth as possible.

"With every journey there will be potholes," Neuheisel says. "The Quarterback Dads become a detriment to their kids when they lose that sense of reality and try to steer clear of potholes. They think they are doing it out of love, but sometimes they are steering them clear of things that are absolutely essential."

Neuheisel mentions Smith, who called his plays at UCLA.

"You have to work through it all," he says. "Homer Smith said of quarterbacking: It's a compilation of pictures in your mind — what defenses you have seen, which receivers are being bracketed, all the problems you encounter. All of those experiences become a mosaic in your head. Use them.

"If you keep getting stewarded away from those experiences — being benched, getting sat down — if you're always looking for the easy way out, you won't be ready when you need to be. Which is crunch time."

Neuheisel speaks from experience. After Washington replaced him following the 2002 season, he took on three new coaching assignments: sons Jerry, Jack and Joe.

Joe played golf at Boise State and nearly qualified for the 2021 U.S. Open at Torrey Pines. As an alternate, he was afforded use of the practice area, and Rick came to San Diego to support him.

Jack, whom Rick coached in youth basketball, played receiver at SMU. Jerry, the spitting image of his father, followed Rick's path as a UCLA quarterback. It wasn't easy.

When Jerry chose UCLA, detractors pointed out it was his only Power Five offer. Neuheisel insisted that his son was worthy of a full ride and that other schools would have closed in if UCLA had not. Whatever the case, the offer reflected Rick's unyielding support.

"When he and I talked, I wanted him to feel like he was the best," he says.

Rick gave Jerry a spot in his 2011 recruiting class at UCLA but got fired that November. His son opted to stay at UCLA and play for Jim Mora Jr., his father's successor.

A career backup, Jerry's "Rose Bowl moment" came in September 2014 when he rescued the Bruins by replacing an injured Brett Hundley against Texas. He completed 23 of 30 passes in the 20-7 comeback win and got carried off the field on the shoulders of his teammates.

Before entering the game, Jerry told Mora he was nervous. As Mora recounted it afterward: "I said: You know what? I'm not. Because I've watched you every day. And I've watched you prepare. And I know how smart you are. And I know your lineage. And I know how your dad taught you."

Neuheisel is now a prominent broadcaster, a CBS Sports analyst who also hosts a daily college football show on SiriusXM's ESPNU Radio.

He coached Jerry in baseball and Pop Warner football, a quarterback turned Quarterback Dad.

Asked for his best advice, Neuheisel recommends that after a tough game, stress the positives and wait to mention any criticisms.

"He will be feeling enough pain already," Neuheisel says. "If it was a great game, revel in it. Allow for the excitement and then critique. It's best to wait until he starts talking about it. If he's down on himself, talk about, one, how he can learn from it; two, why it happened; three, how he can avoid it happening again."

Above all else, sit or stand where no one can hear you: "Because you're gonna say things you cannot believe would come out of your mouth."

CHAPTER 25

THE QUARTERBACK DAD
WITH THE BLUEPRINT

America met "Big Dave" Uiagalalei (oo-ee-AHN-gah-leh-lay) on a fall Saturday in 2020 when son D.J. saved Clemson's season. D.J. completed 30 passes in the Tigers' comeback victory over Boston College, and it seemed the ABC director cut to his jubilant father at least that many times.

"My sister called me during the game and was like: 'Why in the hell are they showing you and not D.J.?'" Big Dave says. "I said: 'Hey, I didn't ask for it.'"

Big Dave didn't so much appear on TV screens as fill them, a 6-4, 380-pound former bodyguard who now has his son's back. Big Dave calls himself a "hype man" for a player who, let's be honest, doesn't need it. And doesn't even want it.

D.J. took the baton from Trevor Lawrence, the first pick in the 2021 NFL draft, and became Clemson's full-time starter. It was a rough ride. Among the preseason favorites for the Heisman Trophy — 11-1 at PointsBet sportsbook — D.J. finished the season with 10 interceptions and nine touchdown passes. The Tigers' production plummeted from 43.5 to 26.3 points per game.

The flip side: Clemson beat Iowa State 20-13 in the Cheez-It Bowl to finish 10-3 with a five-game winning streak. D.J. kept the team on track despite two injuries — a sprained ligament in his left knee that required a brace and injured ligaments in the fingers of his throwing hand.

"My word for this year before this season even started was 'faith,'" D.J. told reporters. "After going through this season, I know exactly why God gave me that word."

Big Dave did not attend the bowl game in Orlando, responding to a Clemson fan's tweet that the decision was "personal" and not a reflection of his feelings toward the program.

His postgame tweet to D.J. went like this: "Son, I'm so proud of you. I'm most proud of how you handled everything. It's not how you start, but it's how you finish that matters most. You still got another year. You have the opportunity to finish strong. I love you son. #UiagaleleiStrong #GodGetsAllTheGlory #GodsPlan."

He retweeted it for those who might have missed it the first time.

That is the essence of Big Dave, a Quarterback Dad who has been advocating for his son since D.J. left the crib — perhaps wearing eye black. When D.J. was 2, his father tabbed him for greatness.

"Just the way he threw the ball back to me," Big Dave says. "Holy mackerel, you know? He looked smooth. Just so you know, I actually had a strong arm too."

To hear Big Dave tell it, he had the size of a nose tackle and the gait of a small forward. His nickname, he says, was "The Halftime Show" because of how he entertained fans at the intermission of basketball and football games.

"At 330 pounds," he says, "I was doing 360-degree dunks."

He shattered playground rims and fired footballs upward of 80 yards. While Big Dave was at West Texas A&M, the basketball coach challenged him to dunk, promising $100 for a two-handed slam. Big Dave says he cocked it back and threw it down while wearing slippers.

Big Dave says that if he'd only had a father like him and a mother like D.J.'s mom, Tausha, "I would be in the league, no doubt. No doubt! My issue is that I was not good at school. I wasn't a bad kid, but school was my struggle."

He grew up in Pomona, Calif., 30 miles east of L.A., playing in summer leagues where grades and transcripts didn't matter. He was eligible long enough to help Mount San Antonio College — "Mt. SAC" in Walnut, Calif. — win the 1997 California Community College Athletic Association championship.

At age 25, his true mission became clear. That's when he and Tausha had D.J., who developed into a beast of a prospect. But in doing so, the family might have created a monster.

"All the success coming to my son, none of this is surprising," Big Dave says. "None of it. I planned it."

Big Dave gets so much flak for his 24/7 social media presence and creation of #BigDavesBlueprint, some have warned him against becoming the football version of LaVar Ball.

Ball is the annoying, self-obsessed, headline-creating showman who once said son Lonzo was better than Stephen Curry and who proclaimed that he, LaVar Ball, could take Michael Jordan. Others see LaVar as a marketing genius, builder of the Big Baller Brand. This much is not up for debate: Lonzo and LaMelo are NBA standouts.

"Look, I respect LaVar Ball," Big Dave says. "But the whole 'he's better' thing and putting a target on his sons' backs ... I would never, ever encourage anyone to do that. I've had people say I'm the next LaVar Ball, and I tell them to shut the hell up. I will never do that and put extra pressure on my sons."

"Never" might be a bit strong considering he also said this during our interview, which occurred before the 2021 season: "When my son gets a whole year under his belt, I will feel sorry for his opponents."

And Big Dave took it to the edge when talking about Lawrence, who went 34-2 as a starter at Clemson and emerged as the NFL's best quarterback prospect since Andrew Luck exited Stanford in 2012.

"People ask me: Who's better?" Big Dave says. "The only reason I give the edge to Trevor Lawrence is because you cannot beat real-time reps. I've never seen a guy with a better arm than D.J. But in a real game, Trevor Lawrence gets my vote."

Now that that's cleared up, let's go back a bit to Big Dave's origins as a Quarterback Dad.

D.J. began playing flag football at 7 and tackle at 9 for the Upland Chargers. But the Pop Warner league assigned players by weight, and because he was so big, officials made him play against older kids. Much older. As a third-grader, he faced sixth- and seventh-graders. Not only that, he played quarterback.

"It was tough that first year," Big Dave says. "You're asking a third-grader to be a quarterback and create time back there. D.J. didn't know. He gets the ball and these guys are tackling him, blasting him. I saw my son at halftime and he had tears running down his face. 'Are you OK, son?' He said: 'I'm all right, I'm good.' That's when I saw the poise. Any other kid would have said: 'I quit! I'm done.'

"Me, I wanted to tackle all those guys hitting my kid. I wanted to ask: 'Where's your daddy at?' I'm that type of dad. I wanted to fight for my son."

You remember the scene in "The Blind Side" when Sandra Bullock's character touts the "protective instincts" of Michael Oher? Big Dave is also a protector. He used his size, vision and strength to guard the likes of DJ Khaled, Meek Mill, Nick Cannon, Rihanna and Chris Brown.

And when D.J.'s Pop Warner coach had him shift to defensive line to move him from harm's way, Big Dave was angry.

"The quarterback who went in was an older kid, a seventh-grader, and he was horrible," Big Dave says.

So D.J. returned to the position, this time as a spread quarterback who had a pre-assigned target. The coach called the play and gave D.J. a specific mission — to execute a handoff, reverse, slant, go route.

"A 9-year-old throwing it 40 yards in the air," Big Dave raves.

And as a pitching prospect, D.J. hit 95 mph.

"I don't want to come off like some boasting father, like my son is better than everybody," he says. "I played football for a long time and with a lot of talented people. I understand when I see something special, and I know how to capitalize on it."

And so we get to the blueprint. The hashtag often accompanies tweets and posts, listed with #GodsPlan, #TheUBrothers and #FamilyIsEverything. Big Dave calls D.J.'s younger brother Matayo, a junior at St. John Bosco outside Los Angeles, a "five-star prospect on both sides of the ball. He got a tight end offer from Alabama and a defensive end offer from Ohio State."

He ranks among the nation's 20 best prospects in the Class of 2023, according to the 247Sports composite.

"Thank you @247sports for upgrading Matayo's profile pic," Big Dave tweeted in December 2021. "My boy looks ready for college right now (6'6" 270lbs). To think I could of (sic) held him back one year. And that means this would of (sic) been his 10th grade year lol. Not fair right? I can't wait to see my son in college."

What defines Big Dave's playbook?

1. **Be a fierce advocate for your son.** If you feel his coach is not using him properly, speak up — especially if the coach's son is blocking his path. Big Dave calls that "Daddy-ball" and says it should not be accepted: "Fight for your kid."

2. **Do not wait for opportunities. Create them.** Big Dave once took D.J. to a B2G Sports camp featuring some of the nation's

top high school players. D.J. joined the throwing line until someone asked: "Who the hell is this?"

B2G CEO Ron Allen walked over and asked D.J. what grade he was in. "Fourth" was the reply. But everything was smoothed over once Allen spotted D.J.'s father. He knew Big Dave from his body-guarding days.

"That is the Big Dave Blueprint to a tee," Big Dave says. "I knew my kid needed that type of challenge."

3. **Leverage his greatness.** (If he, in fact, is great.) A private quarterback tutor told Big Dave he gladly would work with D.J. — at the eye-popping rate of $700 per session. Big Dave replied that D.J. was such a strong prospect, many coaches would line up to work with him for free. The trainer ultimately agreed, waiving his fee.

4. **Create the brand — relentlessly — through social media.** One example: On April 17, 2020, Big Dave tweeted out a birthday wish to D.J. with three photos and a sweet message that included: "I can probably write a book on why I love my son so much." Big Dave then retweeted all the replies. In a two-day span he showcased more than 100.

And here's the rub: D.J. didn't see any of them.

The son has blocked the father on social media. As D.J. put it in a 2019 ESPN.com piece: "I'm like, 'Dad, how many times are you going to post about me?' It's all fun and games, but I don't want to see what they have to say. Not to block them so they don't see me — it's so I don't see (the tweets)."

Tausha said in the same piece: "He might have a target on his back, and my husband doesn't help with all his postings. ... Every now and then,

THE QUARTERBACK DAD WITH THE BLUEPRINT

his brother will tease him or his friends will say, 'Oh, Five-Star's here,' and he'll smile, but it's not what he wants to be called or to be known for."

Big Dave says he's not offended by getting the Heisman from D.J.: "My son blocks me on social media because he doesn't want to see all the hype. I'm his dad, I'm gonna post it. D.J. and Matayo don't want to see it. I don't blame them. They're humble kids. It doesn't bother me at all.

"Look, I know one day my sons will have their kids and they will understand. I'm not gonna stop being a fan. I'm not gonna stop loving my kids. My son knows I love him ..."

Big Dave gets choked up.

"I'll always be there for him," he says. "I tell him all the time: 'I ain't going nowhere, son.'"

For all his hovering, his consistent presence, Big Dave allowed D.J. to choose his high school and college. And both selections were somewhat unconventional. At St. John Bosco, D.J. had to beat out Re-Al Mitchell, a senior bound for Iowa State, to be able to play as a sophomore. He did that, and Netflix was there to document it for Season 2 of "QB1."

Then D.J. selected Clemson, where he theoretically could have had to sit behind Lawrence for two seasons. ESPN.com called D.J. "the country's most patient quarterback."

Says Big Dave: "He went to a high school that already had a great quarterback and people asked: Why are you taking him there? Same thing in college. Clemson had the No. 1 player in the country. Why go there when you could start at 99% of other colleges?

"D.J. understands the importance of waiting your turn. He has never looked for a shortcut. And when it comes to preparation, no one does it better."

Clemson is not the easiest trip from California, though Big Dave loves the drive up I-85 from Atlanta. He can metaphorically stretch his legs, reaching speeds available to Southern California drivers in only the predawn hours.

He vows to continue to attend every Clemson home game. He knows the cameras will find him, a ginormous man and enormous fan of the quarterback wearing No. 5.

"I try not to get the limelight," Big Dave says. "But there's a reason those cameras showed me and people fell in love with me on TV. I'm a guy who genuinely loves his kid. I'm not gonna stop."

CHAPTER 26

THE OLD-SCHOOL
QUARTERBACK WHISPERER

The day Scot Loeffler got his driver's license at age 16, he was 5-10 and 165 pounds.

"Late bloomer," he explains. "No way in hell I would have recruited myself."

But back in the early '90s, the big-time schools didn't expect prospects to be fully formed by their junior prom. Loeffler grew up in Barberton, Ohio, an Akron suburb known for producing future Illinois and Texas coach John Mackovic and industry giant Bo Schembechler.

Loeffler's connection to Schembechler led to early interest from Michigan.

Back then, early meant sophomore or junior year. Michigan coach Lloyd Carr dispatched assistants Cam Cameron and Greg Mattison to woo Loeffler, who was getting nearly as much attention as celebrated Notre Dame recruit Ron Powlus.

Loeffler had no quarterback trainer. He played basketball in the winter and baseball in the spring. He tried to stay sharp by lifting weights with his high school team and throwing on his own. He attended football camps, but their mission was different.

"We actually were taught something," Loeffler says. "They were not just recruiting tools. I went to Bill Walsh's camp (in California) and we got instruction for three or four days. These kids run around the country now to one-day camps to get offers."

Loeffler chuckled about being an "early commit" in 1992.

"It was November 30th of my senior year," he says. "I think the offering process and the taking of quarterbacks as sophomores and juniors is ludicrous, to be honest."

Loeffler's playing career at Michigan effectively ended when he tore his rotator cuff. He planned to go to law school but shifted to student coaching to keep his scholarship. He earned a degree in history and then joined Carr's staff as a graduate assistant, contributing to the Wolverines' undefeated national championship season in 1997.

The quarterbacks: Brian Griese and his young backup, Tom Brady.

It was a strange dynamic considering Loeffler and Griese started as rivals. They met at the aforementioned 49ers camp and didn't quite hit it off.

"Absolutely hated each other," Loeffler says now with a chuckle.

Loeffler was the big-time recruit with a full ride to Michigan. Griese was the standoffish son of Hall of Famer Bob Griese. When Cameron informed Loeffler that Griese had been invited to walk on at Michigan to serve as his competition, Loeffler replied: "Great! I'm going to kick his ass every day."

Turns out Griese had every reason to be introverted. He was still dazed from losing his mother to breast cancer at age 12. With Loeffler sidelined by the shoulder injury, his admiration for Griese grew. So much grit.

"He wasn't very good his freshman year," Loeffler said. "He dropped snaps, he was heavy. A fat quarterback. And he worked his tail off. He became a starter as a senior and a great leader. Super intelligent."

Brady arrived in 1995 and served as the backup to Griese and Scott Dreisbach. In his final two seasons Brady had to fend off Drew Henson, a darling of Michigan fans because of his immense potential in both football and baseball.

Loeffler and his Wolverines teammates believed Brady would be a 12-year NFL pro, perhaps a starter, perhaps a backup, until a moment in spring practice. After Griese struggled, the coaches inserted Brady and the second-team offense against the ones. They went "live," so Brady was a sitting duck.

"They beat the living crap out of him," Loeffler recalls. "They beat his ass and he somehow kept getting up and kept moving the second-team offense. I'm in a sling BS'ing with 'Grease' about what we're going to do that night. We look at No. 12 and say: 'This guy is gonna be a dude.'"

Brady later had to deal with being the second-most popular quarterback on the roster. Loeffler remembers one time when Henson replaced him, and the Michigan Stadium crowd responded with a standing ovation.

"The three worst jobs in the state," Loeffler jokes, "are the goalie of the Red Wings, the coach at Michigan and the quarterback at Michigan."

Loeffler worked at Central Michigan for two seasons and returned to Ann Arbor in 2002 to coach the quarterbacks. A key mission: Persuade Chad Henne, a strong and sturdy Pennsylvania-bred prospect, to choose Michigan over Miami, Georgia, Tennessee and Penn State.

"I recruited Chad for three years and I knew every single thing about the kid and the family," Loeffler says. "I knew he was a fit, an All-Big Ten player, a (future) draft pick."

Henne chose Michigan shortly before his senior season and ranks as the school's all-time leading passer (9,715 yards, 87 touchdowns). He has started 54 games over 13 NFL seasons, most recently serving as Patrick Mahomes' backup in Kansas City.

Loeffler bemoans how recruiting has changed. When he coached quarterbacks at Michigan from 2002-07, Carr would warn him: "You better be on the top juniors."

Now for Power Five coaches, it's freshmen and sophomores. The obsession on both sides — player and school — with committing early invariably leads to poor fits and marriages that do not last.

"How do you (have the time) to do your homework now? How can you project how a 15-year-old kid will be when he's 18?" Loeffler wonders. "It's why you see all the transferring."

Loeffler is now the head coach at Bowling Green after assistant stints at Michigan, Central Michigan, Florida, Temple, Auburn, Virginia Tech and Boston College. He has mentored nine quarterbacks who played in the NFL: Griese, Brady, Henson, Henne, John Navarre, Matt Gutierrez, Ryan Mallett, Logan Thomas and, well, Timothy Richard Tebow. The legendary Gator found it much easier to complete passes in college (67.1%) than the pros (47.9%).

"That (Florida) offense was perfect for Tim Tebow," Loeffler says. "His strength and speed for his size was off the charts and he was super, super competitive. In today's NFL world, with all those RPOs (run-pass options), he'd still be playing."

While at Boston College from 2016-18, Loeffler noticed a dynamite athlete at a camp and offered him a scholarship. Justin Fields even tweeted about it on June 19, 2016: "Blessed to have received an offer from Boston College."

Six months later, Fields verbally committed to Penn State. Then decommitted. Then selected Georgia. Then after sitting behind Jake Fromm, he transferred to Ohio State, where he won the Chicago Tribune Silver Football, which goes to the Big Ten's best player. Now he starts for the Chicago Bears. Few transfer stories end as happily as Fields'.

While at BC, Loeffler did extend a scholarship offer to a ninth-grader, becoming the first Power Five school to promise Kyle McCord a free ride. McCord's father, Derek, played nine games at quarterback for Rutgers from 1990-91.

"It was a no-brainer," Loeffler says of offering McCord. "Big, live arm, accurate and super mature. I talked to his dad and he said: 'Boston College, this is huge.' I laughed and told him: 'Your kid will be able to go anywhere in the country.'"

Less than a year later, McCord, the nation's third-ranked pro-style quarterback (per the 247Sports composite), committed to Ohio State.

What's good about Loeffler's gig at Bowling Green is he doesn't have to waste time trying to romance the fathers of elite 15-year-old quarterbacks. He leaves that to the Power Five coaches and then recruits the ones who fall through the Power Five cracks.

"We sit and wait," Loeffler says. "We do it the old-school way."

Loeffler's advice to young quarterbacks and their dads?

It's the same you see throughout this book: Do not cave to the pressure to specialize.

Donovan Dooley also advocates for that, even though it's better for his business if quarterbacks train year-round: "Go outside to a park and play tag with your friends. Try to make them miss. There is value in that. As a quarterback, you will get to a point where someone on the other side of the line doesn't care about you or family. You're gonna have to get away."

The last word here goes to Loeffler, whose 2021 season at Bowling Green featured extreme highs (a 14-10 victory over Minnesota as a 30-point underdog) and lows (a four-game losing streak in the Mid-American Conference and getting ejected during a win over Buffalo).

Loeffler cautions prospects and their families not to obsess over social media profiles.

"At the end of the day, the colleges will find the true prospects," Loeffler says. "I still believe it's what you put on your high school tape. We also will go see a guy throw live. But this wave of (early) recruiting and early signing, I just don't think it sets up anyone for success."

CHAPTER 27

THE QUARTERBACK DAD
WILLING TO GO BROKE

Adam and Kane Archer have the kind of father-son relationship that allows for moments like this: As they ride home from a game together, Kane remarks that his dad is "probably my best friend in life" before adding an asterisk: "He can get annoying sometimes."

To which Adam replies: "I don't care if he calls me an asshole. We're pretty cool, man. We're a lot alike."

Their relationship is such that the son will send the dad a draft of a tweet before he hits send. What's wild is that the dad will do the same, allowing the son to symbolically wag his finger like Dikembe Mutombo before a tweet goes out.

There is much love between Adam and Kane, who at 13 became the youngest player in University of Arkansas history to draw a scholarship offer from the Razorbacks. If you think that was a fluke, perhaps the home-state school trying to get a PR hit, think again. Over the summer Michigan's Jim Harbaugh called and said: "Kane, we've been watching you, and we want to extend an offer."

The family recorded the call from their kitchen table in Fort Smith, Ark., near the Oklahoma border.

Could Adam have ever imagined Kane, who is in the Class of 2026, receiving offers this early?

"You're gonna catch me sounding arrogant and people will hate me," Adam says, "but yes, I thought it would be this coming spring (of 2022). We've got a possible millionaire baby in the passenger seat.

"Everyone is telling me: 'You've got him lifting weights too young, he doesn't need all the protein, you're living your life through your son, you are consumed by this ...'"

Who gives him a hard time?

"Everyone," Adam replies. "My mom, the other parents around me. You know what it's like being *that* guy? I can understand that their child is a great human being. He'll be a terrific husband one day, maybe a CEO. Well, my son is gonna play in the NFL; that is the card I drew. If they don't understand, that's OK. I'm trailblazing a path and I really don't care what anyone else thinks."

Whoa.

Perhaps Adam is over-the-top in his adulation of Kane. Or perhaps he's just being honest.

He says the following of Kane:

"He is shredded from head to toe; he has an eight-pack."

"His mind is gifted ... and that you can't teach."

"If he had a 'Madden' awareness (rating), it would be very high. I've only seen him take one blindside hit in his entire life."

"Barring injury, I think the kid plays in the NFL."

"Kane was an athlete from birth, fluid in his hips. He just had something that most other kids don't. He also refused to lose. Period. Not an option."

Adam is a bodybuilder and recreational basketball player. He had both of his sons (Cash and Kane) in private training for hoops before their fifth birthdays. Kane began playing tackle football in third grade, debuting as a defensive end.

One time after practice, Kane told his dad: "These kids are not really smart. I'm gonna try to be a quarterback."

How quickly did he take to it?

"It was instant, a duck in water, a natural leadership position," Adam says. "He made everyone better. If they were a 70, he made them a 75 or 80. He helped them understand plays. It was beautiful."

Not long after, Kane scored 10 touchdowns in a youth game with six-minute quarters. At 8, Kane placed his orange cleats in the casket of his paternal grandfather and promised him he would play college football.

When Kane was 10, Adam asked him: What do you want to do in life?

Kane: "I want to play in the NFL."

Want to?

Kane: "I am going to play in the NFL."

Adam says he told him: "If you mean that, as your father I'll do everything to make that dream come true. I'll sell houses, I'll go broke, I'll file for bankruptcy. But I'll have stipulations for you. There will be days when you will absolutely hate my guts. I'm gonna say: 'Get your f**king ass up out of bed!' And I don't want any crying, any excuses. If you're gonna make the NFL, we're gonna have to do it differently from everyone else.

"Do we have a deal?"

Kane says he recalls only some of the conversation. But he remembers the handshake that sealed the arrangement.

Asked about his father's spirit, Kane says: "He's the person in my life who holds me to a high standard. He is trying to do everything to get me right for the next level. Work out. Eat right. No school food for lunch. He makes steak. I get the right amount of sleep. And I go to the gym usually three to four nights a week."

Here's how much Adam trusts Kane: He lets him drive to the gym, a World Class Fitness. That's right. If Adam and older brother Cash are tied up, Kane is permitted to get behind the wheel of Cash's Chevy truck for the short ride.

"He can drive better than my old lady," Adam jokes, adding that Kane, who was born Jan. 21, 2008, already looks like a teenager.

Adam believes driving is safer than biking, mainly because so many drivers are staring down at their phones: "That's like a death wish now."

Kane is on full alert during the drive, saying: "I've seen cops. I just try to act completely normal."

Normal is not a word you'd associate with the Archer household.

Kane's Twitter background recently featured a picture of himself, shirtless, throwing a football (eight-pack … confirmed). Kane not only mentions his football affiliations (Greenwood Bulldogs/KC Outlaws) and height and weight (6'0, 185), he lists his hand size ("10 inches!!"). He includes his coach's phone number, presumably for interviews, and mentions he's the top-ranked quarterback in the Class of 2026.

The website QBHitList.com has it neck-and-neck (or should we say whisker-to-whisker) between Archer and Julian Lewis, a 6-footer from Georgia. Whereas 247Sports.com goes only to the Class of 2024, QBHitList ranks 95 eighth-graders who play quarterback. The 92nd-ranked player on the list is a 5-foot Texan who weighs 90 pounds.

"A lot of smoke and mirrors," Donovan Dooley says of the, um, science that goes into ranking players that young. "They're based on (an analyst) seeing clips versus games. There's no sense of the competition he is up against. A lot of the sites know some dads are willing to pay to get recognized. They're GPCs — good paying customers — who realize that data is important in recruiting."

What effect do rankings like this have on the players? Can they serve as motivation?

"It depends on the kid and his support cast," Dooley says. "It could fuel that fire. But how will he take the recognition? And how will his parents? Parents love recognition … from anything. It's almost like a young lady wanting attention but not caring who it's from. Some dads will use it as a conversation piece: 'According to QBHitList, my kid is No. 7 in the country.'

"They don't realize that the (college) coaches do not care. It's, what can you do for *me*?"

Adam gives Kane some freedom on Instagram. Not so on Twitter, where Kane's 2,500-plus followers include recruiting gurus, national media members and coaches such as Kendal Briles, the offensive coordinator at Arkansas.

"IG is mostly pictures," Adam says. "With Twitter, it's branding."

The father knows how to market people, starting with himself.

He grew up on government assistance. The family paid $165 a month for a mobile home, and Adam worked on farms as the family moved from towns in Texas to Oklahoma to Arkansas. He says his parents were solid — "nobody smoked, no alcohol" — but after they split, Adam stayed with his father.

He took one college class and despised it, taking the advice of a friend who recommended he enter the car business. Adam, you see, could sell rocks to a canyon. His success in the automotive industry has allowed him to purchase 15 rental properties. He now trains employees at a GMC dealership on "how to talk and when to talk. You have to be able to talk to the janitor and the CEO and have respect for both."

He's passing on his media skills to Kane, stressing the importance of "being witty, problem solving and having a ton of common sense."

He wants Kane to build his brand off the field. And to be a leader on it. I bring up Jay Cutler as someone unliked by his Chicago Bears teammates, a quarterback with awful body language. As told to me, shortly after Cutler arrived, the Bears offensive linemen ribbed him until he followed team tradition by treating them to a steak dinner. Cutler sulked so much during the meal, the linemen looked at one another and thought: Why did we bother?

Kane is careful on social media to avoid politics and religion —
or anything controversial — but says that when being interviewed,
"there's no reason to be shy. Be confident like you're talking to a person
instead of a camera."

The Sly Stallone film "Tango & Cash" inspired Adam to chose
the name of his first son. As a friend reminded him: "You're in the car
business. You like money. You like Johnny Cash."

Adam chose Kane Cannon for Cash's baby brother, giving credence
to the idea that the master plan was hatched barely after conception.

"No, just blind luck," he says of the middle name Cannon. "There
was zero intention. He was going to play defensive end. He would
have been a wrecking ball."

Kane taught himself how to throw. And perhaps more impres-
sively, taught himself how to make mechanical adjustments.

He and his dad had a huge argument one day at practice, with
Adam reminding him to keep his elbow up. Kane insisted his dad had
it wrong and stomped off the field crying. A week later he told his dad:
OK, I fixed it.

His dad asked him how.

"I went online," Kane told him. "It was easy. I don't even know
how I was throwing it the other way."

That would not be the final time they butted heads. After Kane's
fifth-grade coach had to step aside because of an illness in the family,
Adam stepped in. Oof, it did not go well.

"I hated every single minute of it," Kane says. "I thought he hated
me. I'd get frustrated and he'd yell at me."

Says Adam: "We fought like cats and dogs. He will listen to me at
home but didn't like me correcting him in front of others. He is down
to taking coaching from anyone on the planet ... except Dad."

Adam would send in a play and Kane would reply: "I don't like it."

To which Adam replied: "Motherf**ker, run the play you're supposed to run! Don't be a little titty baby!"

Looking back, Kane is grateful that time is over. Adam recollects it with a chuckle and a dagger: "We did win it all that year. So he can kiss my ass."

Adam is the quintessential modern Quarterback Dad when it comes to private trainers, saying: "We traveled the country looking for one. Nobody could captivate me."

Until they were in Dallas for a camp and listened to a trainer from 3DQB, which focuses on functional strength, mechanics, motion analysis, management skills and nutrition. The trainer is John Beck, a middling NFL quarterback from 2007-2012 who is now one of the hottest names in the industry. His client list includes Matt Ryan, Dak Prescott, Jared Goff, Carson Wentz, Justin Fields, Zach Wilson and Trey Lance.

"Within three minutes," Adam recalls, "I said: 'That's our guy. Where is he from?'"

California.

"Shit!"

What was Adam saying about his willingness to go broke?

CHAPTER 28

THE OFF-THE-CHARTS QUARTERBACK DAD

By now you've read about the quarterback who received an offer from the University of Michigan at age 13, the one who began publicizing his hand size at 12 and the energetic tyke who designed his own logo at 11. As baby boomers get older, football flingers get younger.

How much younger?

The next generation of Quarterback Dads quickly transitions from potty training to quarterback training. Not long ago, Donovan Dooley noticed that a man from Detroit, Jamal Doggett, mentioned Quarterback University on social media. Doggett wrote that he had registered his son, Josiah, for a group training session.

Dooley was intrigued. He got in touch with Doggett. But not before he scrolled through the Instagram handle @dual_threat_qb2_jd. There he saw a Quarterback Dad in a category of his own. The pictures display an adorable kid barely bigger than some of his trophies. There's a compilation video, set to Meek Mill's "Dreams and Nightmares," that uses pictures and clips to tell the story of Josiah's speedy recovery from an elbow injury.

The captions: "Doctors said take 4 weeks off, no throwing, no workouts. Just rest."

Then we see an image of Josiah getting a consoling hug from his dad: "I figured this would be the end of my season knowing that I had high hopes."

And then, against a black screen: "My daddy said you wanna give up? Or come back stronger?"

Next: "What do you think?"

And then there's Josiah, using a mini-trampoline to run in place. Doing curls with bands. Taking snaps from Dad. Doing step-ins on an agility ladder. Running around cones. All this to the title on the post: "Now or Never." Without a hint of irony.

At the time, Josiah was 5. Five! And doing kettlebell workouts.

At 6, there's video of him jump-cutting around a dining room chair. And a photo of him flexing with the caption: "Got my work in! Did you?!?!"

So Dooley should not have been surprised by what transpired during his first conversation with Jamal, who said of his son: "He is not your average 7-year-old."

Dooley is reluctant to train kids that young. They might not be mature enough to handle instruction. Some are more inclined to stare at the clouds. But Dooley felt comfortable enough to give this one a shot. He handed off the Doggett duo to Kyle Short, one of his instructors.

In their first conversation, Doggett told Short: "I've just got to alert you, Coach. Josiah, he ain't no normal 7-year-old. He's advanced!"

Doggett asked Short whether the coach was on Instagram. Yes, he replied. Then Doggett began sending him clips of Josiah throwing passes — in customized cleats with his preferred No. 2. (Matching the number his father wore as a high school baseball player and running back/cornerback.)

Short examined one of the photos, asking himself: "Hold up. Is that a fake tattoo arm sleeve?"

Turns out that is one of Josiah's signature looks. Many noticed it on social media and thought the ink was real.

"It's his trademark now," the father says.

Doggett coaches running backs at Grosse Pointe South High School, and one of his players recommended the sleeve, saying: "This will look sweet on your son."

When the Doggetts showed up for Josiah's first workout, Short noticed the boy wearing a jersey and headband with his custom cleats.

"Where is the sleeve?" Short asked, half-serious.

"That's only for game day, Coach!" Josiah replied.

At his first session, Short asked Josiah to introduce himself to the fellow quarterbacks.

"Waddup," he replied, as some chuckled. The kid has swag! And that was all he said.

Short asked: What school do you attend?

Josiah froze.

But he showed poise during the workout. Short said Josiah was "locked in" and brash enough to try to steal reps from the older kids by cutting them in line.

"He listens, he's very coachable and his confidence is through the roof," Short said. "He looks the part when he's throwing and has a good base. He's way ahead of the curve. Then again, to be honest, I don't have a ton of people to compare him to."

As a Quarterback Dad, Doggett is in a league of his own when it comes to social media. He posted a nearly three-minute sizzle reel of a Josiah throwing session on Facebook with the message: "I told myself I wasn't gonna post this and just keep this to myself! But f**k it, people gonna love it, people gonna sneak diss … The progress my son has made makes me proud! Still putting in the work day in and day out!!! Love you Josiah! I don't own the rights to this music."

During Josiah's first few training sessions with Short, Doggett stood within earshot of the action, filming every rep. After the second workout, Short said that so long as the father did not physically get in the way of a drill, he was OK with his proximity and incessant recording.

A couple weeks later, Short said Doggett was "inserting himself into the training. He is physically showing frustration on his face and forcefully moving Josiah's body to the stance I'm telling him. After the session, the father will tell the son: 'Man, I'm telling him the same things you're telling him. But he doesn't do it.'"

The Demonstrator Dad. No. 8 on Dooley's list.

Asked if he has to fight the urge to get involved, Jamal texted: "Kyle's sessions are nothing but amazing! I love it so much! It's worth it!"

Indeed, quarterback training is not cheap. The Doggetts opted for a package of two on-field workouts and two Zoom sessions (one focusing on pass protection; the other on reading defenses) per week. Cost: $600 per month. On days without quarterback training, Josiah goes to speed training with his track coach. That is provided for free.

It's all part of the father's grand plan.

He said he initially noticed talent from Josiah when he was 3 and wearing his first jersey — a onesie. The father was impressed with his son's wrist action. At 4 they started playing catch, and Josiah began running laps.

"No time off and look where we are now," he said. "When Josiah turns 10, that's when the spotlight will be on him."

Josiah is already a national champion and All-American in his dad's eyes. Literally. Playing in the West Seven Rams Youth Club, Josiah led his 6-and-under team to a title at Detroit's Ford Field in October. That prompted this Instagram caption: "Make sure you call me champion when you say my name!!"

Doggett said one of the coaches for a rival team offered the family $1,000 to switch allegiances. They passed.

Another Instagram post shows Josiah, on a phone, with his arm extended. He is displaying his championship ring. You'd almost think it's a parody account. Doggett said he doesn't worry about overdoing it on social media because he knows he's not hurting anyone.

And here's a reflection of how much Doggett loves his son. He works the "midnight" shift as a computer technician for Ford, installing software in F-150 trucks, from 10 p.m.-6 a.m. He's up with Josiah at 7:45. He sleeps and then takes him to practice or speed training in the afternoon. Then it's homework, putting Josiah to bed and getting ready for another eight-hour shift.

Asked how far he thinks his son can take football, Doggett replied: "Straight up honest, I think he is probably going to make it to the NFL. The doctors say he will be at least 6-3. He's already a big boy — 83 pounds and he just turned 7. With the right mechanics, he can go far."

Perhaps you're reading this and thinking: STOP! Let the kid be a kid.

But here's some good news for those concerned: Doggett insists he does not force Josiah to play or practice. He gave him a week off from throwing after the fall season.

"I will never push him to his limit; I let him do whatever he wants," he said. "He's excited when it's time to go to Dooley. He asks me: Dad, is it football practice yet?"

And Doggett said he and Josiah are super close: "Absolutely, I can talk to my son about everything. And he opens up to me."

Short remains a bit conflicted on whether it's wise to have a kid as young as Josiah in training. What advice would he give parents?

"I would tell them that in extreme and rare cases, yes, if the kid loves it and you as a parent are supporting your kid, go for it," he said. "But if the kid is 7 and I start hearing about college scholarships and playing on Sundays, that would be crazy talk."

You want crazy talk?

Early in 2022, Dooley was contacted by a Quarterback Dad in Michigan in search of private training. The kid is advanced, the dad promised. He's poised. He can focus.

Also, he's 5 years old.

Dooley politely declined. But the Quarterback Dad refused to take a knee.

"He offered," Dooley said, "to pay in cash."

UPDATES ON TWO OF OUR FAVORITE QUARTERBACK DADS AND SONS

Envision this: The year is 2036 and the Bears' starting quarterback is Trae Taylor, a six-year NFL vet. It's game day in London. Super Bowl LXX.

When Taylor was 12, quarterback trainer Mike Hohensee said his greatest hope was to watch Trae on NFL Sundays: "Just leave me some tickets at will call. I'm willing to pay for tickets to watch … but don't make me."

The Taylors do not leave tickets for him. They split with Hohensee early in 2021 after nearly four years of live sessions, film analysis and mentoring, a longtime professional quarterback sharing his wisdom with a prodigy. It speaks to the delicate nature of the parent/trainer relationship. One day a Quarterback Dad puts his trust in him; the next he's declining to reply to his texts.

The split with Hohensee occurred after Steve Wilson, the quarterbacking Yoda, shared a new follow-through technique with Trae and his father, J.R., that addressed his trajectory. Trae incorporated it into a workout and misfired on about half of his slant throws.

No big deal, right? The kid was 12 and trying something new.

But it led to a schism after Hohensee commented on his low completion percentage and J.R. thought: We don't want any negativity in the building. Donovan Dooley did not have a business relationship with Hohensee but was fine with Hohensee continuing to work with Taylor. But J.R. and Trae favored a split, re-establishing Dooley and Wilson as Trae's coaches.

Taylor and Hohensee never talked it out. Hohensee continued inviting Trae to sessions, but the Taylors declined to appear.

Trae continues to thrive. He selected Carmel Catholic High School, an hour north of Chicago. His Facebook recruiting page is loaded with images of MVP trophies and yoga poses, an ambitious travel schedule with past visits to campuses such as Michigan State and Miami.

It also contains this telling post from J.R. on Dec. 4, 2021: "I have had to make some hard decisions. Who Trains Trae, what high school will he go to. We talk about a team, a Circle, that is so tight from friends and coaches. The one decision I'm so thankful we made was saying ok, QBU is it. Coach Donovan Dooley is it. Little did we know that the decision would give him such a team behind him, that even if Trae decided he didn't want to play football anymore, his future is still so bright. MI (Michigan) is our 2nd home because that's where the extended family is. And the future and men that will enter Trae's life will also be amazing."

Hohensee believes he served Trae well, saying: "I didn't coach that kid soft, I coached him like he was my son and we got great results. I see his highlights when other kids post stuff (on social media). The impressive thing is, he is calling his own plays ... the whole game.

"He's a special talent, an NFL kid in my mind, no doubt."

You'll recall that after five-star recruit Brock Vandagriff verbally committed to Oklahoma, the family attended a 2019 game in Norman. The school celebrated a touchdown by sending its beloved horse-drawn wagon onto the field. But the Sooner Schooner crashed after making a sharp turn, freeing the horses and littering the field with debris.

The Vandagriffs, already wary of selecting a campus nearly 1,000 miles from home, took that as a sign. Brock decommitted — and then faced the wrath of keyboard warriors on anonymous message boards.

"You want to respond like Liam Neeson in 'Taken,'" said his father, Greg. "I have a particular set of skills ..."

Funny how things turn out. Had Vandagriff chosen Oklahoma, he would have lost his head coach after one season, as Lincoln Riley left for USC. Had he selected Florida, also in his top three, he would have lost that head coach, Dan Mullen, to the firing line.

What were the odds that both Oklahoma and Florida would hire new coaches after the 2021 season?

"About a million to one," Greg estimates.

Brock selected his hometown school, Georgia. Greg and wife Kathy were thrilled to keep him nearby, but they had reservations. In 2019, Georgia QBs threw for just 223 yards per game. The next season they completed a combined 58.2% of their throws.

"Kelly and I said: 'Are you sure?'" Greg recalled.

After Brock replied that he can be successful in any scheme, Greg told him: "OK, we will trust the process."

Fast-forward to Jan. 10, 2022. Downtown Indianapolis. Greg and Kelly, wearing Georgia gear, take a selfie in front of Harry & Izzy's steakhouse, where a giant banner heralds the national championship game. They take another picture of the Lucas Oil Stadium video board when Brock appears, his name in giant block letters.

By the end of the night, Kelly is wearing a ballcap that says NATIONAL CHAMPS. And she, Greg and Brock are holding up their forefingers. No. 1!

"I don't talk a ton about my faith," Greg says. "But I can tell you, God saved us on this one. He protected us from ourselves."

It was a dreamy finish but not a dream season for Brock, who was fourth string behind walk-on turned hero Stetson Bennett, former five-star recruit JT Daniels and pro-style prospect Carson Beck. Vandagriff saw the field in only two games, firing one pass against Charleston Southern.

Ten years ago — heck, maybe five years ago — little thought was given to true freshmen supplanting accomplished vets. But now when a five-star recruit doesn't play immediately, fans wonder what went wrong and start scanning the transfer portal. Even with a national championship team.

Greg, a highly successful high school coach, also had to fight the urge to show concern, saying: "As a dad and a coach, it made me step back. It's not what's best for my son, it's what's best for the team. This is where you do *not* want to fill your son's head with crap like: If they don't give you 10 plays a game, we need to 'portal' out of this. I needed to sit on my hands and let my son flounder. Let him experience the ups and downs from the bottom of the rung without trying to manipulate it."

Vandagriff went up against Georgia's top-rated defense as a member of the scout team, earning praise from coach Kirby Smart in November: "He's really athletic, makes throws on the run, is very accurate and competitive. He doesn't always have the best protection."

But he gets a ton of support from home.

Although the 24-year-old Bennett said he would return in 2022 for his bonus COVID-19 season, Greg is not assuming that his son will ride the bench again this fall.

"Spring football," the Quarterback Dad says, "will be interesting."

ACKNOWLEDGMENTS

Teddy Greenstein

This is my first book, so forgive me for being clueless. After I committed to writing *Quarterback Dads* in the fall of 2020, I figured it would take me six months. (Hey, it'll be like writing a dozen feature stories for the Trib.)

I thought: Cool, I'll knock this out and then give my friend Joel Boyd a weekend to edit it. Slap on a cover, off to the printer and voila! Umm … no.

Turns out producing a book is a massive undertaking. In addition to my partners — private quarterback trainer Donovan Dooley and a financier who wishes to remain in the huddle — we started with a project manager, Todd Zimmermann. He is a longtime family friend and the brains behind the "Oliver the Ornament" series, which was selected three times by the First Lady to be read at Children's National Hospital at Christmastime. He became our "coach."

It helps to have the world's best designer, which is what Charlie Wollborg's business card should say. If you've seen our cover or website (QuarterbackDads.com), I think you'll agree. We enlisted some wonderful attorneys to advise and help with trademarks and copyrights. Thank you to Howard "Nat" Piggee, Tom Levinson, Neill Jakobe and Jennifer Cormier (Ropes & Gray LLP), along with publishing vet Eric Lupfer and audio maven Tylere Presley.

Thanks to my former editors at the Chicago Tribune — Amanda Kaschube, Colin McMahon and Chrissy Taylor — for green-lighting the project. Shout-out to my bosses at PointsBet (Johnny Aitken, Ron Shell, Kyle Christensen, Rick Martira and Liam Rocklein) for betting on me.

My friends in the media world were clutch, sharing cell numbers and advice: Michael Rosenberg, John Bacon (i.e. Teddy's dad), Pete Thamel (also Teddy's dad!), Rob Elder, Dave Revsine, Bruce Feldman, Stewart Mandel, Ian O'Connor, Sam Farmer, Matt Rudy, Lars Anderson, Dan Snierson, Jim Gray, Pete Sampson, Dan Wetzel, Pat Forde, Adam Rittenberg, Matt Fortuna, Ivan Maisel, Chuck Culpepper, Mike Hall, Rick Pizzo, Rachel Nichols, K.C. Johnson and David Meltzer. I owe beers and wings to my eagle-eyed team of Jimmy Greenfield, Kevin Ding and Michael Lev. Tip of the cap to Jeff Pearlman, whose Substack and podcast are the Bible (OK, Torah) for a first-time author.

Thanks to Brad Glanzrock for my back-cover mug shot and to Len Mead for hiring him. And to my OGs (in alphabetical order): Paul Behar, Mike Carbone, Henri Cauvin, Matt Craner and Dave Straker. And I can't forget New Jersey's finest — Jennifer & Dory Altmann, Rebecca and Jonah, the true football expert of the family.

Big thanks to those I interviewed: Archie Manning, Todd Marinovich, Warren Moon, Big Dave Uiagalelei, Jay Barker, David Peters, Phil Rochelle, Greg Vandagriff, Rick Neuheisel, Carl Williams, Jamal Doggett, Brady Quinn, Joel Klatt, Pat Fitzgerald, Bret Bielema, Scot Loeffler, Kirk Ciarrocca, Chris Batti, Mike Hohensee, Ron Veal, Dan Persa, Kyle Short, Steve Wilson (as featured in "The QB Mentor"), Allen Trieu, Greg Biggins, Tom Lemming and Steve Wiltfong.

And to the families: Phil and Chris Simms, Kurt and EJ Warner, J.R., Hilary and Trae Taylor, Peyton and Doug Ramsey, Jay and Bryce Underwood, Ross and Drew Viotto, Trent and TJ Green, Jim and J.J. McCarthy and Adam and Kane Archer.

Almost done, I promise! But back to the team. I know the math on this doesn't work, but Dooley has become a lifelong friend. I only wish I had a son with a rocket arm to hand to him. His mother, Ella, was a delightful interview.

Fantastic to reunite with the aforementioned Joel "Superstar" Boyd, who has had the misfortune of reading/editing me since we were 18. His eyes are so sharp (and heart so full of the Georgia Bulldogs), he knew ESPN.com missed a 2021 game in which Brock Vandagriff played. And thanks in advance for PR help from Adam Fluck, who will help me blanket (haunt?) Chicago's airwaves.

The final acknowledgement goes to my core: Nori, Elle, Emmy and Bo, our Australian mini-labradoodle. Yes, I just thanked a dog.

Donovan Dooley

Traveling the world to train quarterbacks seems like a fun gig, but it has its ups and downs. The gratification comes from impacting young men across the country and watching their dreams come true. The downside comes when you spend more time with other kids than your own.

My family's sacrifice is unmatched. My wife Tiffany is my team-mate. We talk in football lingo in our household. We huddle up, we call audibles, we run "check with me's", we have "kill" calls (to get out of bad plays). We limit turnovers and move the chains. We just WIN. We worry about "What's Important Now."

Our kids (Bri, Donnie, Riah, Ari and Cannon) have taken a back seat to Quarterback University. This passion – or should I say, obsession – with football fuels our family. Genuine relationships have been built with clients over the past 10 years.

I was diagnosed with cancer in December 2019, and it changed my life forever. I got the call on Friday the 13th and was told to report to the doctor within three hours. Surgery and radiation would be required. While on bed rest, I tried to calculate how long I'd be off the field. I informed all of our clients that I'd be away for a bit to take care of my health. Guys, let me tell you how God works: Literally EVERY personal client continued to pay his or her monthly tuition. It's a testament to the commitment level of our families and friends.

My late father (William), mom (Ella), and brother (Pip) have supported me through every endeavor since I can remember. When I told them I had this "Quarterback Dad" vision in 2015, they couldn't see it. But the more they saw the interaction between Dads and their sons at our camps, it became clear "what time of day it was." I smile as I write that.

I genuinely want to thank EVERY person that played a part in making this come true. Our team is awesome! Side note: My baby boy Cannon turned 1 on June 25, 2020. My wife bought him an inflatable target for throwing footballs. He has football socks, hats, pajamas … and I named him Cannon! So I wonder: Am I a Quarterback Dad? Is Tiffany a Quarterback Mom? Time will tell (smile). Love you guys!

CPSIA information can be obtained
at www.ICGtesting.com
Printed in the USA
BVHW042151200423
662786BV00020B/174

9 780578 399775